MAVERICKS

MAVERICKS
A Gallery of Texas Characters

GENE FOWLER

University of Texas Press
Austin

Requests for permission to reproduce material from this work should be sent to:
Permissions
University of Texas Press
P.O. Box 7819
Austin, TX 78713-7819
www.utexas.edu/utpress/about/bpermission.html

∞ The paper used in this book meets the minimum requirements of ANSI/NISO Z39.48-
1992 (R1997) (Permanence of Paper).

Library of Congress Cataloging-in-Publication Data

Fowler, Gene, 1955–
    Mavericks : a gallery of Texas characters / Gene Fowler.—1st ed.
        p.   cm.
    ISBN 978-0-292-71834-0 (cloth : alk. paper) — ISBN 978-0-292-71819-7 (pbk. : alk.
paper)
        1. Eccentrics and eccentricities—Texas—Biography.   2. Texas—Biography.   3.
Texas—History—Anecdotes.   4. Texas—Social life and customs.   I. Title.
    F385.F625   2008
    920.076409'04—dc22
    [B]   2007027201

For my son, Nate, the songman

Contents

CONTENTS

Part Two: Other Texas Characters

Appendixes

Acknowledgments

In addition to the people and institutions mentioned in the text and photo captions, a muchas gracias goes out to the following for assistance with this book: Lewis Lee, Webb Gallery, Betty Heath, Martin Delabano, Bill Crawford, Tyler Beard, Dorothy Leach, Fort Worth Public Library, Drew Julian, Ann Gallaway, Jill Lawless, Mike Murphy, Jack Lowry, Lori Moffatt, Nola McKey, Marty Lange, Jane Wu, Anne Cook, Nancy Bryan, Leslie Tingle, Laura Griffin, Bill Bishel, Theresa May, William Lewis Williams, Jean Price, Elvis Fleming, Travis Whitehead, Fort Sam Houston Museum, San Antonio Public Library, Tarleton State University Library, Charles J. Rike Memorial Library, Carl Strickland, Kenneth Garrison, the Brush Country Museum, Diego Domingo, and especially to the marvelous Gyla.

Show business is a tough town.

—ANDY KAUFMAN

INTRODUCTION

Sintesi Texana

"This state loves a maverick," proclaimed Texas gubernatorial candidate Kinky Friedman in 2006. "Always has."

Texans invented the maverick. According to the story that seems the most plausible, the term entered the American lexicon on the state's coastal plain in the mid-nineteenth century, when Samuel A. Maverick, then a resident of Matagorda County, accepted a herd of four hundred cattle as payment for a loan. As the stock was allowed to roam free and unbranded, unmarked strays found in the area were generally described as "one of Maverick's." The situation continued—and the name stuck—after Sam moved the cattle to his San Antonio ranch and then sold the herd, leaving the buyer to round up strays from several adjoining counties.

In time, explains David Dary in *The New Handbook of Texas*, "the term *maverick* came to refer to any living creature, human or otherwise, that goes its own way rather than acting as part of a group or herd." The word's application may have expanded beyond its original Old West context, but it's still the best definition I've seen of the Texas character, both historical and contemporary. It definitely applies to the individuals gathered in this book.

Active from the frontier era to the space age, these one-of-a-kind Texans inhabited the worlds of oil, ranching, real estate, politics, rodeo, metaphysics, show business, folklore, and art. Many of the folks assembled here might be seen as occupying that cultural niche of the American psyche known as the "eccentric Texan." A couple of them indulged their whimsy as prime examples of the archetypal "eccentric Texas millionaire." Most savored a quirky "sense of place" on far fewer resources. Many of the more inscrutable mavericks profiled here strike me as folk artists who worked in the wide-ranging medium of performance art.

"It's all right to lie about Texas," proclaimed Commodore Basil Muse Hatfield, "because it'll be the truth tomorrow." Indeed, the art of fiction has long been a primary element of the Texas character. The urge to make up a story in order to transcend a more prosaic circumstance (or for any number of other reasons) appears deeply woven into the region's moral fabric. Many, of course, would not view such expressiveness as lying. It is rather that time-honored tradition of stretching the blanket. Redecorating the facts.

To some Texans, describing an individual as eccentric can be just as offensive as inferring that the person is not on speaking terms with the truth. In 1958, for instance, a Houston matron wrote to *Dallas Morning News* Texana columnist Frank X. Tolbert, complaining about his characterization of Martin Parmer as the "eccentric old-time Texan for whom Parmer County is named."

"I come to a slow boil," wrote the Houston history buff, "every time I think of you calling poor Mr. Parmer, one of the signers of the Texas Declaration of Independence, an eccentric. What do you base this on?"

If a certain history of Livingston County, Missouri, penned in 1886 had been handy, the lady might have boiled more quickly upon reading that even nineteenth-century show-me-staters had considered Parmer "an eccentric character." Before heading for Texas in 1825, Parmer served in the Missouri legislature, where he informed fellow statesmen that he was "a Ring Tailed Painter [Panther] from Fishin' Creek, wild and woolly, hard to curry. When I'm mad, I fight, and when I fight, I *whip*. I raise my children to fight. I feed 'em on painters' [panthers'] hearts fried in rattlesnake grease."

Like beauty, eccentricity is most readily identified in the eye of the beholder, though it is perhaps even more difficult to define. Dr. David Weeks, an American neuropsychologist based in Scotland, attempted to shape a definition in 1984 after noticing that three of the four leading textbooks on psychiatry did not address the eccentric personality. The fourth text, Dr. Weeks wrote in his 1995 book, *Eccentrics: A Study of Sanity and Strangeness* (co-authored with journalist Jamie James), identified eccentricity as a form of "predominantly inadequate or passive psychopathy," and further stated that it is "usually difficult to distinguish the symptoms of eccentricity from schizophrenic manifestations."

Perturbed by such haphazard clinical observation, Dr. Weeks began analyzing the whims and ways of eccentric individuals in the British Isles and the United States. While acknowledging the subjective nature of his subject, Weeks' analysis of voluminous data collected in the study identified a number of traits shared by more than a thousand individuals, both living and dead, who were examined and determined to be, or to have been, eccentric. Interestingly, Weeks concluded that, in general, eccentrics were happier and healthier—both mentally and physically—than eccentricity-challenged folks.

The five most important and common characteristics identified by the neuropsychologist's study are, perhaps unsurprisingly, nonconformity, creativity, curiosity, idealism, and a happy obsession with "one or more hobbyhorses." To a lesser degree the eccentrics were generally found to be intelligent, opinionated, aware of their uniqueness from early childhood, and to possess a "mischievous sense of humor." The data also suggested that the percentage of "classic, full-time eccentrics" living amongst us is somewhere between one in five thousand people and one in fifteen thousand people. As a lifelong resident of a region that has proven such a fertile breeding ground for eccentrics, I would have estimated a much higher percentage.

• • •

One steamy August night in 1976, I stood in an Austin convenience store parking lot and watched a man pour large bottles of Coca-Cola into the radiator of his Lincoln Continental. The man wore a cowboy hat and a sheepskin winter coat, and he chuckled elfishly as he muttered something about his Continental's fondness for imbibing the soda water.

A snippet of out-of-the-ordinary activity framed in my memory, the replayed scene began to exhibit the formal qualities of an art piece. In its brevity and topsy-turvy reality, it possessed some of the characteristics of the *sintesi*, a performance form developed by the Italian avant-garde movement, active from approximately 1909 to 1933, known as futurism.

In *Futurist Performance* (1971), Michael Kirby notes that the *sintesi* form was "very short and non-naturalistic." The works "ranged in style from symbolist and didactic to alogical and nonrepresentational. In them can be found the origins of Dada, surrealism, and theatre of the absurd." Over the last several decades the form has also been one of the myriad influences that shaped the eclectic phenomenon that has come to be known as performance art.

Expressed in perhaps the broadest of terms, a fundamental objective of much twentieth-century art and art theory was to encourage a greater awareness of the omnipresence of aesthetic experience, to explore the thin and often vanishing line between art and life. After contemplating some physical or visual expression of minimalism, for instance, in the formalized, exalted setting of a museum or gallery, one might perceive the same sculptural richness in, say, the architecture of a highway overpass or hay bales dotting a field. Similarly, a choreographic dimension may be suggested by the most mundane of movements. Random sound, any sonic phenomena, might achieve the character of an organic musical performance. In an unexpected moment, a fractured narrative may offer a mirror to one's own fragmented perception of reality. An everyday environment might suddenly flush with a heightened, cinematic quality. And it's in that intersection of art and life, where the frame dissolves and encompasses all, that performance art is often created and perceived.

In her 1979 book on the subject, curator and critic RoseLee Goldberg asserted that "by its very nature," performance art "defies precise or easy definition beyond the simple declaration that it is live art by artists. Any stricter definition would immediately negate the possibility of performance itself. For performance draws freely on any number of references—literature, theatre, drama, music, architecture, poetry, films, and fantasy—deploying them in any combination." In a 1980 issue of the Los Angeles art magazine, *Dumb Ox*, artists Allan Kaprow and Paul McCarthy offered an encyclopedic list of the developmental sources of performance art:

> futurism, Dada, surrealism, happenings, events, actions, body works, land art, conceptualism, environmental and action music, absurdist and structuralist theatre, concrete and action poetry, the dance of everyday movement, film, video, architecture, arts criticism . . . as well as outside art proper in radical politics and feminism, spiritual disciplines and rituals, education, spectacles, public demonstrations, sports, and the social sciences.

In the quarter century since those descriptive attempts were made, the concept of "performance art" has assumed a wiggly presence in mainstream culture—partly due to the medium's proliferation in the 1970s and '80s and to extensive media reports of the withdrawal of NEA funding from some purportedly shocking artists. Thus, it has not been uncommon over the last twenty years or so, when encountering someone or a group carrying out some unusual activity, for the observer to comment wryly, "Oh, that must be performance art."

Some years ago, for instance, a young insurance salesman from the Great Lakes area went to a Dallas Cowboys football game at Texas Stadium in Irving dressed as a Dallas Cowboys cheerleader. The man stole onto the field and managed to join the gals in a little cheerleading before security wrestled him to the ground. Previously, the insurance salesman had donned a professional baseball team uniform and hung out for a while in the dugout during a game. If this man had advanced his unusual hobby as a performance project—perhaps with a component of research on gender roles in sports—it would quite possibly be enthusiastically received and accorded a deserving credibility within the reference of at least some sectors of the contemporary art world.

Or take the case of Monsieur Mangetout (Mr. Eat It All), who appeared in Amarillo in 1979 to eat a waterbed as a promotional event for a local merchant. Mangetout was then scheduled to go to Tokyo and eat a helicopter. I was doing clerical work in a contemporary art museum when I discovered Mangetout and fantasized about the curators inviting him to come and eat some of the less appealing items in the museum's permanent collection as a performance event.

An episode in which mainstream media sought to gently mock (or perhaps to pay homage to) performance art was planned for the Congress Avenue bridge in Austin shortly before the bombing of the Murrah Federal Building in Oklahoma City in 1995. In response to Sallie Jacque's avant-garde performance on the bridge entitled *100 Beds*, John Kelso, humor columnist for the *Austin American-Statesman*, announced plans for his own performance piece, *100 Lazy Boys*. The performance would have featured 100 recliner-potato males drinking beer and performing maneuvers in their Lazy Boys, but was postponed out of respect for the victims of the bombing. The art community has awaited a rescheduling ever since.

Performance, in the perspective employed here, encompasses everything from formal presentation in an art-world environment to actions, projects, and situations in the "everyday" world that somehow transport participants and audiences to an enhanced mode of experiencing the everyday. Citing the work of sociologist Erving Goffman as an influence, notably his 1959 book, *The Presentation of Self in Everyday Life*, Jens

INTRODUCTION

Hoffmann and Joan Jonas propose in their 2006 book, *Art Works Perform*, that "culture—in particular the connection between ritual practice, staged situations, and the overall process of civilization—is now viewed as performance."

Hoffmann and Jonas observe that in the last few decades several "common terms, such as 'body,' 'identity,' 'multiculturalism,' or 'gender' . . . have been used repeatedly as a means of classifying performance-related work." Artists have tortured their flesh and had themselves shot as sculptural activity. They have posed for extended periods of time as the opposite gender, as invented selves in both fictive universes and the "real" world, as persons living in a previous century. Some have publicly explored their sexuality in manners both beautiful and grotesque. Others have ripped into raw, intimate territory and shared their naked humanity as political statement. A surprising number have felt compelled to inform the world of their fetish for condiments.

Much of the more compelling contemporary work involves several and sometimes all of the elements identified by Hoffmann and Jonas. The performances of Guillermo Gómez-Peña, for instance, resemble anthropological exhibitions in which Gómez-Peña and associates present themselves as part-Mesoamerican, part-futuristic border-crossers in "living dioramas," where they are costumed as "CyberVatos," "ethnocyborgs," "transgender mariachi cyborgs," "Zapatista strippers," "El Mexterminator," "El Naftaztec," "Border Brujo," and other hybrid entities. Their work often explores the ironies of cultural tourism. "Through the performance ritual," Gómez-Peña explains, "the audience vicariously experiences the freedom, cultural risks, and utopian possibilities that society has denied them. Audience members are encouraged to touch us, smell us, feed us, defy us. In this strange millennial ceremony, the Pandora's box opens, and the postcolonial demons are unleashed."

The work of German artist Joseph Beuys (1921–1986) explored similar cultural demons. In his 1974 action, *Coyote: I Like America and America Likes Me*, Beuys lived in the René Block Gallery in New York for several days with a coyote. "The Texas wolfhound represents pre-Columbian America, which still knew the harmonic living together of man and nature, in which coyote and Indian could live together with one another before they were both hunted down by the colonialists," wrote critic Caroline Tisdall of the piece. As Beuys sought to establish a connection to the coyote and the animal urinated on copies of the *Wall*

Street Journal, the installation–performance took on an anthropological context. "The represented environment," Tisdall concluded, "must effect the modern consciousness originally, archetypally, and beyond the times."

"Art alone makes life possible," Beuys stressed in an interview with Canadian artist Willoughby Sharp. "I demand an artistic involvement in all realms of life . . . I advocate an aesthetic involvement from science, from economics, from politics, from religion—every sphere of human activity. Even the act of peeling a potato can be a work of art if it is a conscious act."

The same impulses and perspectives are seen in the subconscious forces that drive artists we commonly describe as "self-taught," "outsider," "folk," or "vernacular." In catalog notes for the 1997 exhibition, *Spirited Journeys: Self-Taught Texas Artists of the Twentieth Century,* curator Lynne Adele notes that the 1980s and '90s witnessed a sharp increase in public awareness of "self-taught" artists. While noting that many artists work in a gray area between the "academically trained" (or those who perhaps were not academically trained but found inspiration and acquired ability in an art-world perspective) and the "outsider" artists, Adele established practical criteria for exhibition selections. The curator chose artists "whose work represents a unique vision and style developed on their own, uninfluenced by other artists, trends, or formal art traditions," artists whose works "document their unique and sometimes eccentric views of the world, and yet somehow speak to the viewer in a universal language."

That's largely the way I feel about Bobcat Carter, Governor Willie, Cyclone Davis Jr., and many of the other mavericks profiled here. Their "unique vision and style" compelled them to express "their unique and sometimes eccentric views of the world" in actions, events, lifestyles, and other forms that suggest the perspective of performance art. Bozo Texino and George Ray may be seen as performance folk-artists who more clearly utilized traditional visual arts (drawing and environmental installation). Others explored the nature of identity in intriguing ways that reaffirmed the Texas tradition of reinvention of the self, established by such marquee eccentrics as Bigfoot Wallace and Judge Roy Bean. Commodore Hatfield's love affair with the Trinity River could be interpreted as a land-art project. And I can't look at the magnificent frontiersman's suit created by Texas pioneer Robert Hall without thinking of the performance attire worn by Dadaist Hugo Ball at the Cabaret Voltaire in Zurich circa 1916.

The political performances of Cyclone Davis Jr., Governor Willie, and Bicycle Annie seem to presage the art campaigns of 1976 California gubernatorial candidate Lowell Darling and 2006 Texas gubernatorial candidate Kinky Friedman. Darling—who carried a fat rubber hand on a stick, with which he shook the hands of California voters—proposed the elimination of all jobs and a thirty-thousand-dollar annual stipend for citizens "just for being themselves." To achieve such a budget, Reverend Ike, the colorful radio evangelist and prosperity consciousness pioneer, would have been put in charge of California's finances. All billboards in Darling's California would have been moved to one location that motorists could drive through like an animal safari park. (The artist ultimately polled some sixty thousand votes.) Friedman, of course, is the only candidate for governor in Texas history who sold an action figure depicting himself. The most difficult aspect of Kinky's campaign for many voters was deciding whether he was running in the "real" world or the "art" world.

The distinction can be even more problematic in subtler, more nuanced performances. And performance art can sneak up on a person in such a manner that the demarcation between art and life simply evaporates.

In the 1990s, I began to notice a woman repeatedly standing by the side of the road in Austin on one random day after another. Swathed and cloaked and hooded in fabric and other materials that draped her still figure with a strange foreboding, she stood with a blank, disturbing gaze that glared through passing motorists. I wondered intently about Why and What. There was a troubling presence in the countenance, a sense of alien expression. I felt oddly conflicted about making eye contact, gawking. Some days it seemed as if she were defying those who traveled the road to look directly into her harrowing visage. On other days, to look seemed a required rite of passage. At times, passersby wondered if the woman suffered from some misbehavior of the mind. At other times, she seemed to possess a power that transcended such menial differentiations.

At some point it dawned on me that I hadn't seen her for a while. And then one day she was there, in the newspaper, her obituary, a photo of that transfixing gaze. I was surprised to read that it was Helen Mayfield, an artist and dancer with whom I had been slightly acquainted in the 1970s when we had both been members of a loose-knit artist collective. The review of her life's course noted that she had worked as an arts and crafts counselor at Austin State Hospital, where she inspired the well-known, self-taught artist Eddie Arning to begin painting. Her encouragement led to Eddie's release from the institution, which allowed him to spend "the last 30 years of his life in freedom and creativity." And then I read:

> In recent years, many university-area observers enjoyed her unique and ephemeral performances as a walking art form in splendid costumes which she had designed and constructed from ordinary materials . . . As beautiful and misunderstood as a wild mustang, she now runs free.

• • •

Portions of the introduction appeared in *Contemporary Art/Southeast,* Atlanta, in 1980.

MAVERICKS

PART ONE

A GALLERY OF PERFORMANCE FOLK-ARTISTS

I

Commodore Hatfield

Prophet of the Trinity

One blazing August day in 1933, about one hundred citizens gathered at the Belknap Street bridge over the Trinity River in Fort Worth. As the Bluebonnet String Band played "Over The Waves," the Trinity's foremost prophet and promoter, Commodore Basil Muse Hatfield, waved his Stetson at the crowd and embarked for Chicago on a twenty-four-foot flat-bottom boat called the *Texas Steer*. At every chance on the trek along inland waterways, promised the commodore, he would bend folks' ears about the wondrous river "more fertile than the fabled Nile acreage." Furthermore, the 62-year-old commodore vowed that until a Trinity River canal connected Cowtown with the coast and made the growing Metroplex an inland port, he would cease practicing the tonsorial arts.

A wiseacre or two in the crowd that day cackled that the *Texas Steer* would not even make the thirty miles to Dallas on the snag-laden river. But Commodore Hatfield, convinced that the best way to prove a waterway navigable was simply to navigate it, finessed his craft of river-bottom cypress on a remarkable American journey. Powered by a hiccupping, one-cylinder motor, the *Steer* floated down the Trinity to the Intracoastal Canal, then up the Mississippi, Missouri, and Illinois rivers to the Windy City. Puttering into the World's Fair Lagoon, the *Steer* looked something like an elongated Conestoga wagon on water. Chicago dubbed Hatfield the "Texas Scowboy."

With the commodore stopping along the way to preach the Trinity gospel, the Fort Worth-to-Chicago round trip took twenty-one months. When he came chugging back down the Trinity in May 1935, sporting Old Testament whiskers and locks, the commodore proclaimed that he'd given 459 public testimonials about his beloved river. Dozens of brass bands and public officials had greeted Hatfield and his ever-changing crew along the route, and the portly commodore had especially enjoyed some sixty-four banquets. Twice, he appeared in Christmas parades as jolly Saint Nick.

Shown here in 1935 with a county sheriff named Cecil Watson, Commodore
Basil Muse Hatfield spent the last eight or nine years of his life promoting the
Trinity River. Earlier, Tibetan lamas had taught Hatfield patience by instructing him to transfer sand from one bucket to another, one grain at a time. Courtesy of the *Fort Worth Star-Telegram* Photograph Collection, Special Collections,
the University of Texas at Arlington Libraries, Arlington, Texas.

Fort Worth welcomed the Texas Scowboy home with a Main Street parade, five hundred bucks, and a new Stetson. Though promoted by the chamber of commerce to honorary First Admiral of the Trinity, Basil Muse seemed to prefer the rank of commodore the rest of his life. "They used to call me Colonel," the commodore liked to say. "You know, the kernel is the inside of the nut."

But the name was Colonel Hatfield when many Fort Worth residents first heard of him in a 1932 front-page story in the *Fort Worth Press*. Reporter C. L. Douglas happened by as Hatfield—in a minor *tour de force* of performance folk-art—was attempting to have a telephone installed in his "outdoor office," an eight-inch gap between the Hotel Texas and the Worth Building that he had claimed by "squatter's rights." When the phone installer protested, Hatfield lamented the loss of Americans' sense of humor and led reporter Douglas around the corner to his "reading room," a bay window near a newsstand. There, as the busy world passed by, the commodore uncorked the tale of his adventurous life.

A day or so later, the newsstand owner pointed to the *Fort Worth Press* front page and exclaimed, "Hey, ain't that you?" Pulling out his horn-rims, the commodore focused on the headline: SQUATTER'S RIGHT CLAIMED FOR 8-INCH OFFICE SPACE—"COLONEL" HATFIELD TRIES TO HAVE TELEPHONE INSTALLED ON SIDE OF BUILDING.

The peculiar sensation of getting his name in the papers appealed to Basil Muse Hatfield, and the notoriety would come in handy when he later went whole-hog for the Trinity Canal. There were hordes of daily scribblers in Texas in those days, and between his great World's Fair voyage and his death in 1942, the commodore intrigued and enchanted a great number of them.

With minor variations, the scribes each gathered a similar Hatfield saga of globe-spanning action. Most noted that river navigation ran in the commodore's veins—his grandfather, Basil Muse Hatfield, a veteran of the Battle of San Jacinto, had piloted steamboats on the Trinity and the Brazos. Commodore Hatfield, according to a 1987 interview with his grandson, Basil Muse "Bill" Joblin, was the twenty-seventh family member to be named Basil Muse (sometimes spelled Bazil Muse). Born on a plantation at Washington-on-the-Brazos on July 4, 1871, Commodore Hatfield grew up with tutors and reportedly taught school himself as a young man. In 1941, he reminisced in an uncharacteristically cranky manner for *Dallas Morning News* reporter Paul Crume. "They wouldn't let me play with boys I wanted to," the commodore fussed. "I allus liked a one gallus kid. They'd beat the devil out of me and cuss me back. All the boys I got to play with was too polite."

Escaping the too-polite side of life, young Basil Muse took to the road. By one account, he sailed at age sixteen on a cattle boat for England, then accompanied a party of British scientists to the Orient. In another, a twenty-something Basil took off for South America on a four-master. Most agree that he took up arms for the English in the Boxer Rebellion in China and also in the Boer War in South Africa. In the latter conflict, Hatfield was reportedly awarded the Victorian Cross, but the Texan declined the honor, insulted Queen Victoria, and was jailed for a time. As the commodore liked to say, he was a temporary guest in many of "the world's best jails."

His adventures also included, the commodore told the scribblers, serving in the Spanish-American War, helping to engineer construction of the Trans-Siberian Railroad, hunting for ivory and mining for diamonds in Africa, and prospecting for oil in India, Persia, South America, the Balkans, and Alaska. In Tibet, Hatfield told newsman Dean Tevis, lamas taught him patience by instructing him to transfer sand from one bucket to another, one grain at a time. Many observed that, due to his travels, the commodore was adept in Eastern philosophies. "Live now, in this minute," the bearded sage would offer, punctuating his advice with a booming laugh. "Yesterday has gone, and, good or bad, you can't do anything about it, and tomorrow is a myth. Reality lies in this minute alone. The eternal now."

The 1910s found him mining silver in Mexico. There, the tale tells, he crossed paths with the likes of Tex O'Reilly, Pancho Villa, and General Christmas. Landing on the wrong side of a regional uprising during the Mexican Revolution, the wandering son headed for home. In the '20s, the commodore later told the press, he took to the oil fields and became wealthy. But as Dean Tevis reported, "Oil brought the commodore afoul of the law." Hatfield apparently spent a few months in federal prison before they booted him out with an executive pardon. "Federal authorities, the story goes, wanted to make a test case of charges against him," wrote Tevis. "He bucked at that, pleaded guilty, to the prosecutor's chagrin, and refused a parole. The commodore was like that."

The exact nature of those charges remains unclear, but Hatfield told

The Texas Steer stops in Beaumont as Commodore Hatfield greets local officials. Courtesy of the *Fort Worth Star-Telegram* Photograph Collection, Special
Collections, the University of Texas at Arlington Libraries, Arlington, Texas.

Commodore Hatfield visits with more folks along the Trinity. Courtesy of the
Fort Worth Star-Telegram Photograph Collection, Special Collections, the University of Texas at Arlington Libraries, Arlington, Texas.

Paul Crume that he was drilling for black gold in the giant East Texas field in 1932 when he collided with the government proration program, which limited the amount of oil pumped, thereby promoting conservation and price stabilization. In a life-changing epiphany, wrote Crume, the commodore realized that "he had no business in a LaSalle automobile." He sold the fancy car, got out of the "money-grubbing" game, and determined to find ways to help his fellow man in the grips of the Great Depression.

The quest soon led to the Trinity, explained Crume, "brown with mud, swampy and boggy, draining a region which, if it hadn't everything on earth, had the stuff to make it out of." As the commodore put it, "I decided to make 'em recognize that river in no damned uncertain kind of way."

And recognize it folks did. When the Texas Scowboy returned from his World's Fair trip, he toted a big stack of newspaper clippings, all featuring his bearded visage and Trinity River rhapsodies. As Paul Crume put it, the commodore was "as full of torrential words as Walt Whitman." Hatfield continued making news up and down the river the rest of his life, commanding attention with an aura that suggested a combination of spiritual dignity and worldly gusto.

"At first," recalled H. B. Fox in the *Houston Chronicle,* "people stared when the commodore came along, and the commodore knew it. The way people looked at him as he strode along, his beard and hair flowing in the wind, was a constant source of amusement to him."

"I'm not so crazy," the commodore would often profess. "Who in thunder would pay any attention to me if I shaved?" He encouraged others to cultivate facial forestry as well. "You will find it as cool as a mountain stream trickling down through a sylvan retreat," he purred. "It's something about the accumulation of moisture in the underbrush and subsequent evaporation as the gentle breezes are wafted through the luxuriant whiskers . . . I'm as cool around the neck as an earthworm burrowing its way through moist ground shaded by fern and fed by a spring."

The commodore's daughter, Sue Hatfield Joblin, observed years later that, after her father got Trinity fever, she didn't see him nearly as often. (Of the 1930s and '40s news reports examined, no mention is made of the commodore's family until son Bill went missing in action during World War II.) Apparently, Commodore Hatfield lived on the *Steer* much of this time. Often, he rambled the Trinity valley on foot, taking his rest under leafy canopies. "It's good for the body," he explained. "Every tree is an oxygen tent. The human body [has] its own thermostat, if you'll let it operate. My body adjusts itself to the weather, because I don't pamper it too much." When staying indoors, the commodore avoided fires. "A fire will soak all the grease out of your body and you'll go outside and catch cold," he continued. "The same is true with bathing. There are times when a man should take a bath, and others when he should resist with all his strength. But you got to know your own thermostat to handle the matter and still be a sociable creature welcomed where men foregather in groups in a close room."

Sowing words of hope up and down the Trinity basin, Hatfield was a welcome supper guest in hundreds of homes. In town and out in the country, his appetite became as famous as his beard. Michael Landon of Dallas, whose family often hosted the commodore, later recalled the river prophet's favorite repast of a pound of bacon and a dozen eggs. In a 1972 *Texas Star* article, Fred Frank Blaylock noted an old saying about the Scowboy's dining habits that revealed a surprising note of commodore-sized moderation: "One chicken is not enough, but a turkey is a little too much."

Beaumont historian John H. Walker testified to Hatfield's prodigious consumption of vittles in a 1993 article in *Texas Highways* in which he recounted a mid-1930s trip up the Trinity with the commodore on a twenty-four-foot workboat. The river prophet undertook the trip to promote barge traffic on the waterway, but to Johnnie Walker and his friends, it was a grand adventure. "The river was beautiful," he recalled, "with huge oak and pecan trees hanging out over the stream and the water almost crystal clear."

On the second day, the inland mariners unknowingly passed a prison farm, where a half-dozen armed men on horseback appeared on the riverbank. The sight put a scare into the younger crewmen, Johnnie wrote, because "we were not sure that these weren't some of the ghosts from the commodore's swashbuckling past." Campfire tales of their leader's "experiences as a soldier of fortune" turned out to be Walker's favorite part of the trip. The commodore talked most about adventures in South American coups and revolutions with "freebooters" like William Walker. "He recounted a couple of times that he and William

Walker were captured by an armed force and were scheduled to be shot by a firing squad," wrote Johnnie, before some unknown party bought their freedom with bribes.

Hatfield also regaled his crew with stories about old Texas, when steamboats puffed up the Trinity. Some of the young men might have been a bit skeptical until they arrived at the ruins of a set of locks, built in the nineteenth century to aid the boats' passage. "That was the trouble with the commodore's stories," Johnnie observed. "They had a habit of turning out to be true."

The river party turned back after five days, in the vicinity of Midway and Madisonville, and headed back toward Liberty when a hard rain began to fall. The low overhead of the Trinity bridge at Liberty awaited their return, which only took one day with the river's flow. When they reached the bridge, their boat's mast was one foot taller than the bridge's lower beam. "Fortunately, however, the problem was easier to solve than it first appeared to be," Johnnie recalled. "We just moved the commodore and his three-hundred-plus pounds over to the side of the boat, and he tilted the boat just enough to let the mast slide by."

Fort Worth economics professor Floyd Durham observed in his 1976 book, *Trinity River Paradox*, that the commodore "covered the Trinity Valley with the thoroughness of an expert geologist." He preached the importance of soil conservation in the same breath that he called for the river's canalization and encouraged folks to more actively market the lignite, potash, sand, gravel, numerous varieties of abundant woods, and other resources along the Trinity basin. "Texas is the richest yet most undeveloped place in the world," he emphasized to Dean Tevis, "but she's got to dig and fight for herself just like old Sam Houston and my grandfather Basil Muse Hatfield did at San Jacinto. It's hard to get people aroused, but they will be."

In 1940, the commodore and other members of the Forward Trinity Valley Association founded the Trinity Valley Chemurgic Institute in Romayor, a town hard-hit by the Depression that was sometimes called "the capital of Poverty Valley." As the name suggests, the institute offered studies in the industrial use of organic matter such as Spanish moss, castor beans, and acorns. The nation's entry into World War II apparently ended the school's brief operation, and according to Fort Worth Hatfield chronicler Orville Hancock, a flood washed the log cabin laboratory away in 1942.

In 1941, the commodore took to calling himself Senator Hatfield when he tossed his Stetson into the ring in the special election called to fill the U.S. Senate seat of Morris Sheppard. It must have given the commodore a measure of satisfaction to see his name and picture in national magazines. *Time*, calling him "old Basil Muse Hatfield, Commodore of Inland Rivers, who is campaigning for a five-ocean navy," ran his image next to that of fellow candidates Congressman Lyndon Johnson and border-radio magnate/goat-gland rejuvenation surgeon Dr. John R. Brinkley. Under the headline, "27 Seek Senate Seat in Screwy Texas Race," *Life* published a photo of the commodore emitting a cloud of cigarette smoke, with a caption noting that he favored the "organization of a lottery" to pay for his five-ocean navy. Other candidates pictured include E. A. Calvin of Houston, "a lifelong foe of taxes" who campaigned wearing only a wooden barrel in reference to cartoonist Will B. Johnstone's taxpayer, and Cyclone Davis Jr., another maverick who earned his own chapter in this book.

Senator Hatfield explained that he was announcing his victory before the election: "If you don't count 'em ahead of time, you might not ever have any votes." In the end, after spending $8.25 on his campaign, the commodore polled twenty-six votes. (One might make a case, however, that he would have been a better senator than the election's winner, Texas Governor W. Lee "Pappy" O'Daniel.)

That September, feeling that the Trinity canal was assured, the commodore clipped his locks and trimmed his beard into a neat Van Dyke. Though Hatfield denied submitting to the scissors because his chin shrubbery had become a fire hazard, Frank X. Tolbert reported that "the commodore smoked Bull Durham cigarettes to the stubs in absent-minded fashion, and he was always setting his beard on fire."

The commodore was walking the banks of his beloved river one day in 1942, searching for more materials to add to his list of natural resources, when he fell and sustained injuries that led to his death. His last request sought to take him down the Trinity once more. "When I die," he said, "I don't want any weeping at my funeral. I want my body cremated and the ashes sprinkled into the Trinity River. And don't play any funeral dirges. I believe in action. I want some snappy music at my funeral, like 'My Bonnie Lies Over The Ocean' or 'Turkey In The Straw' . . . nothing sad . . . I just want folks to remember, there was a man who was willing to make a fool of himself if he thought it would help his fellow man."

• • •

The hope that the commodore's son, missing in action in World War II, might be found alive and return home for the ceremony delayed the Trinity prophet's last trip down his river until the summer of 1987. Daughter Sue Hatfield Joblin was touched by the crowd that came to pay respects, even though most hadn't known her father. Dr. Barry Bailey of Fort Worth's First United Methodist Church described Hatfield as "a man of vision." Major John Rigby of the U.S. Corps of Engineers echoed those words. "Some people say he was an eccentric," said the major. "I say he was a visionary to envision the importance of the resources of the Trinity."

And *Fort Worth Star-Telegram* reporter Janice Johnston noted that, true to the commodore's request, a band played "Turkey in the Straw" and "My Bonnie Lies Over the Ocean."

2

Cyclone Davis Jr.

"Bewhiskered Dervish"

Despite interesting performances in the last couple of decades by Clayton Williams, Ross Perot, and a few others, the Texas political scene of late seems, well, a little dull. Whither has fled the earthy, theatrical magic evidenced by Ma and Pa Ferguson, Lyndon Johnson, Cactus Jack Garner, and so many others? It makes one long for the day when Texas politicians called each other skunks, buzzards, termites, grub worms, and human ants.

With the exception of the political performance artist/gubernatorial candidate Kinky Friedman, the current crop of public servants and candidates makes me wish we had a performing bearded prophet like Cyclone Davis Jr. When Cyclone died in 1954 at age seventy-three, just a few months after his final campaign, he had run for governor, lieutenant governor, U.S. Congress, and U.S. Senate. But the only elected office he ever captured was mayor of Rotan, located about fifty miles northwest of Abilene, in 1906.

Cyclone Davis Jr. ran for almost every office in the state, but the only race he ever won was for mayor of Rotan in 1906. Courtesy of the Texas/Dallas History and Archives, Dallas Public Library.

Asked why he continued to run in the face of incessant defeat, the self-proclaimed "bewhiskered dervish" said that running for office gives a person vision for greater things. Cyclone was indeed blessed with the "vision thing." He was a vibrant activist for concerns of the aged. Calling himself the "Texas Bank Wizard," he masterminded the first bank "named for, owned by, and operated by cowboys," also in Rotan. At other times, Cyclone introduced himself as "the best durned fender repairman in Texas."

But the most likely reason why the candidate who pitched himself to voters as "an able and interesting Editor, Lecturer, Poet, Cowboy, Author, Athlete, Actor, Organizer, Politico, Builder, and Banker" ran for office is simply because he enjoyed it. During his 1950 campaign for lieutenant governor, Cyclone led a snake dance through one North Texas town. His 1952 gubernatorial campaign literature featured a photograph of himself dressed as Saint Nick with the slogan "Nobody Snubs Santa Claus." A Corpus Christi newspaper described one of his last appearances at a rally in Belton: "They cheered the most for old Cyclone Davis, 73, with his long white beard and waving arms, who didn't need one of those newfangled public address systems to get his message out."

The bewhiskered dervish was a pioneer proponent of recycling. While running for the Senate in 1941, he set up a shop under the Cadiz Street viaduct in Dallas where he collected thousands of tin cans which he converted into shingles, fences, and other decorative articles to sell to raise campaign funds. The shop and office were made of discarded packing cases where visitors often found a sign—"If Not In, Am Out Campaigning."

Born in 1881 in Mount Vernon, in Franklin County, Cyclone Jr.'s given name was Arlon Barton Davis. His parents, Belle Barton and James Harvey "Cyclone" Davis Sr., had tried to name him Anson, after the West Texas town where his uncle C. D. Davis had founded the *Texas Western* newspaper. But pied type spelled it Arlon, and Arlon it was.

Cyclone Davis Sr. was a populist organizer and U.S. congressman before World War I. A Kentucky newspaper dubbed him "A Texas Cyclone" in 1894 for his tornadic oratory, black sombrero, frock coat, flowing beard, and stomping boots. He later made "Cyclone" a legal part of his name.

The original Cyclone could have taught today's politicians to sling

F.ve Minutes With Texas' Next Able Governor
1952

Thirty Years Ago

1937

ARLON BARTON CYCLONE DAVIS
Nobody Snubs Santa Claus

Name, A-R-L-O-N, accidental formation of pied type. Reverse N-O-L-R-A was given his son.

Printers devil in childhood, America's youngest; Newspaper Editor at sixteen, Cashier of Bank at 20, President a Chamber of Commerce and The Blanco National Bank at 23, Mayor of Rotan at 24.

From 1900 to 1926, successfully organized and operated twenty-five Texas Banks. Resurrected, and for three years successfully resuscitated and operated the United States Trust and Savings Bank (unincorporated) of San Antonio. As chairman and President, he developed unusual and unique franchise privileges to operate and maintain a system of private banking throughout the United States and friendly foreign nations continuing for twenty one years after his death.

Is Co-author, joint owner and editor of his father's famous book; MEMOIR BY CYCLONES DAVIS, the only book ever printed to have five dollars paid one thousand or more times before publication and delivery.

Managed successful campaign and was clerk of Cyclone Davis, Congressman-at-large, during the Wilson Administration.

Executive Vice President, joint owner and editor, Sherman Courier, sixth in the seniority role of Texas newspapers. The elder are Galveston-Dallas News, San Antonio Express, Vicoria Advocate, and The Belton Journal.

Unabashed by Washington society, despite his rugged individualism — as an East Texas hill billy, he paid fourteen dollars rent on a full dress costume, to attend President Wilson's second wedding.

Founder protagonist and life president of TEXAS FOUR HUNDRED CLUB, a state-wide organization of outstanding patriotic and intellecqually minded women.

Heroically though unsuccessfully, he staunchly thrice supported Tom Hunter for governor, and since the age of twenty-five has been importuned to become a candidate. The only man in America nominated five times in five months for governor of a state (Texas) and forbidden to run ONCE.

He was the first to write a letter of suggestion and encouragement to John Nance Garner to become a candidate for President.

Founded and put into operation the first flood light systems for football, baseball and all nocturnal sports in Texas. Was joint owner of the finest lighted miniature golf course in existence.

Champion in salesmanship of four hundred hand picked accredited business executives; members San Antonio Chamber of Commerce.

Is an able and interesting Editor, Lecturer, Poet, Cowboy, Author, Athlete, Actor, Organizer, Politico, Builder, Banker; optimistic, vigilant and determined. Has spoken to over 1,000,000 students in Texas, and 500,000 outside during 1938.

Judge Chas. E. Coombes of Stamford sent him a telegraphic invitation to attend the Cowboy Christmas Ball at Anson; primarily because of his organization and presidency of the Cowboy State Bank and Trust Co., of Rotan, the first to be named for, operated and owned by cowboys. All home capital, subscribed verbally, paid in, charter filed, and temporary building housed fourteen thousand dollars in deposits in one day before a residence was built in the town.

WHO'S WHO IN FINANCE has the following to say of him:
Davis Arlon B.—Banker, Editor, Author: Born Mt. Vernon, Franklin County, Texas, Feb. 7, 1881. Eldest son of James Harvey (Cyclone) and Belle Barton Davis. Married, New Braunfels, March 25, 1907, to Cora L., youngest daughter of Mayor and Mrs. Chas. Alves. Children; Nolra Earl, Louise Belle and Cecyl Charlsie. His father was a prominent politician; national organizer of the populist party, Commissioner of Indian Affairs under Grover Cleveland, official lecturer Farmers Alliance Federation and Knights of Labor; co-founder Texas Press Association 1882, its third president 1885. Colleague of William Jennings Bryan and nominated for vice president with him at Sioux Falls

At sixteen, Arlon managed and edited the Alliance Vindicator of 3500 circulation. He cut cord wood to acquire an education in Commercial Law Bookkeeping, Court Stenography Public Speaking, etc. Held intercollegiate state championships; running broad jump, poll vaulting, tennis singles and doubles and basket ball. Was catcher on Addran T. C. U. baseball team. Became a resident of Rotan and a leader in community activity of Central West Texas: Mayor, President Rotan Chamber of Commerce, The Cowboy State Bank, Western Loan and Guaranty Co., Central Texas Gun Club and Fisher County Tennis Association. Manager Cowboy Opera House. Democratic Chairman; Christian (Disciple); Member Texas Bankers Association (Seconded J. W. Butler's nomination for President) Treasurer Rotan Independent School District; Official Court Reporter; and designated Depository of Fisher County. Registered the first automobiles in Comal and Fisher Counties and among the first in Texas.

Cyclone Jr. produced some of the most interesting campaign literature in Texas political history.

CYCLONE DAVIS

THINK AND LIVE - VOTE AND VENTURE *President*

AMERICA'S YOUNGEST:
EDITOR,
MAYOR,
BANK AND CHAMBER OF COMMERCE PRESIDENT
PERENNIAL,
POPULAR,
PROMISING,
PROGRESSIVE,
DEMOCRATIC,
DRAFTED, LABOR
PEACE,
PENSION AND PROSPERITY
CANDIDATE

Friends Of The Aged Council

ARLON BARTON CYCLONE DAVIS

PRESIDENT: Corporate Floodlight Company, Texas Amalgamated Club Congress, Texas Four Hundred Club. and a Texas Comedy; "Fun-Incorporated." President: Friends of the Aged Council, Texas Pension Association and the Sherman Courier. National Chairman: American Brotherhood of the Brush Clubs, Mascot of the Boneheads.

339 W. Brooklyn, Dallas 8, Texas, 1953

Phone WO-1031

"TWAIN CYCLONES"
(Our Movie Title)

BY REQUEST OF ONE HUNDRED THOUSAND NOTARIZED PETITIONERS FOR GOVERNOR SUBJECT DEMOCRATIC PRIMARY, 1952.

CYCLONE DAVIS
A World Thinker

APRIL 18, 54.

FIVE TIMES
ILLEGALLY
BLACKED OFF

339 W. BROOKLYN
DALLAS 8, TEXAS
A World Builder

ADVOCATING THE C. H. C. ANDERSON PLAN: SIXTY DOLLARS OVER SIXTY FOR EVERYBODY RICH OR POOR.

HON GEORGE HINSON, CANDIDATE FOR LIEUTENANT GOVERNOR, MINEOLA. TEXAS.

DEAR FRIEND GEORGE:-- THE BRAIN WASHING, DARK AND SINISTER SHROUD OF BLACK OUT, KNOCK DOWN AND DRAG OUT, IS AT THE HOME PLATE NOW.

FOUR COLUMNS OF PREDATORY PELF DEALING FOR THAT JELLY BEAN, BEN RAMSEY AND HIS PAL SHIVERS, AND JUST A FEW LINES RELATIVE TO YOUR OWN CANDIDACY, FROM TODAYS TWO DALLAS DAILIES, CLIPPINGS OF WHICH I SEND YOU HEREWITH, ALSO A FILE COPY OF MY LETTER TO OUR LITTLE TIN HORN REPUBLICAN GOVERNOR, ALLEN SHIVERS, OF THE SIXTEENTH, COPY OF WHICH I DELIVERED IN PERSON TO THE TIMES HERALD, WHICH FOUND ITS WAY SPEEDILY TO THEIR OVERBURDENED WASTE BASKET.

WITH SIX HUNDRED PEOPLE PAYING MY FILING FEE FROM EVERY STATE IN THIS NATION, THE DOMINION OF CANADA, HIWAIIAN ISLANDS AND THE TERRITORY OF ALASKA, I AM NOT EVEN CONSIDERED A CANDIDATE, AND NEITHER WILL THE VOTERS, DRIVEN LIKE SHEEP BEFORE A TRAINED COLLIE, CONSIDER EITHER YOU, ME, OR ANY OTHER TRUE AND TRIED FRIEND OF THE PLAIN DOWNTRODDEN, AND LONG SINCE FORGOTTEN, "JOHN Y. PUBLIC," UNTIL AND UNLESS THE UNTHINKING, APATHETIC AND INDIFFERENT RANK AND FILE RALLY TO THEIR OWN DEFENSE BY THE FORMATION OF A "PEOPLE'S SLATE OF CANDIDATES" TO BUCK THE SHIVERCRATIC GANG, THAT ARE GOING TO TEAR DOWN THE FLOOD GATES OF HEAVEN AND RAISE THE GRASS ROOTS OF HELL TO PERPETUATE THEIR RUTHLESS, RECKLESS AND RUINOUS STAMPEDE TO PERPETUATE THEIR FIVE YEARS OF STRAGLE HOLD, WITH A HOGTIED, HAMSTRUNG AND HOBBLED GRIP UPON THE ELECTORATE.

JOSEPHAS SAID TWO THOUSAND YEARS AGO: "WHEN THE ENEMIES OF THE PEOPLE, BY FRAUD, DECEPTION AND LEGERDEMAIN, SHALL HAVE GAINED WEALTH AND POWER, AND TASTED THE S W E E T N E S OF IT, IT IS NEXT TO IMPOSSIBLE TO WREST THAT POWER FROM THEIR CONTROL." LET'S WREST IT!!!

SINCERELY, *Cyclone*
CYCLONE DAVIS.

Cyclone was still givin' 'em hell shortly before his death in 1954.

damp earth with greater gusto. "He may be a human jackal," Cyclone Sr. roared of one opponent. "He may be a son of the devil, although to call this aggregation of insolence, this consummate image of depravity who moves about the sacred chambers of our legislative hall with moral putrefaction oozing from his hide a child of the devil would be to wrong the devil.

"He may be a skunk who, in the lottery of life, got two legs instead of four. It may be supposed that he, like the toadstool, simply exuded as a foul and fungus growth from some den of infamy and darkness, where he lived in boon companionship with a gruesome gang of thugs, sandbaggers, and fallen women, before he was commissioned by the syndicated interests to turn the slime pit of his lecherous personality upon my distinguished colleagues and myself."

Though he lost his seat in Congress in 1916, a defeat he attributed to "booze, boodle, and big business," Cyclone Sr. was also politically active late in life, announcing in 1934 at age eighty that he intended to run for governor.

Before his father died in 1940, Cyclone Jr. announced his intention to run for governor, squaring off against Hillbilly Flour magnate and radio personality W. Lee "Please Pass the Biscuits, Pappy" O'Daniel. Cyclone Jr. campaigned dressed as Uncle Sam, vowing to "eat earthworms, drink branchwater, and sleep on Johnson grass to frighten this granddaddy taxation spider away." But in the Democratic primary contest, Cyclone came in sixth in a field of seven.

The following year, 1941, the bewhiskered dervish jumped into a crowded special senate election occasioned by the death of Senator Morris Sheppard. "27 Candidates Seek Senate Seat in Screwy Texas Race," giggled the headline on a photo spread of contenders in *Life* magazine. The portrait of Cyclone showed him gazing reverently skyward, and the caption identified him as a "squatter-sage" who lived in his recycling shop underneath the Dallas viaduct. "I don't need to campaign," Cyclone told *Life*. "Providence will place me in the Senate."

The two Cyclones published two of the most peculiar books ever penned by public figures. Cyclone Sr.'s *Memoir* appeared in 1935, followed by Cyclone Jr.'s *Offings and Musings of A. Nutt* in 1937. Both volumes present considerable challenges for the reader. *Memoir* is a collection of Cyclone Sr.'s speeches, sprinkled throughout with inscrutably miscellaneous odds and ends. The book's final paragraph, labeled "Explanatory," states, "The reader may be confused by the multiplicity of apparently disconnected articles and illustrations foregoing, but in reality each has a bearing either through lasting ties of friendship, personal contact, or unusual experiences with the author, editor, or their colleagues."

Offings and Musings of A. Nutt is filled with poems, riddles, jokes, cartoons, odd bits of wisdom and commonsense instruction, pictures of friends and public officials, an essay on grass, and peculiar doodles and illustrations. The cover features drawings of WFAA cowboy singer Peg Moreland, and characters named Professor A-Corn, Mr. Peanut, and Miss Pickon. "With 400 years of glamour and 6,000,000 people," Cyclone Jr. had printed on his book's cover, "not 400 Texans have written books of 400 or more pages. THIS IS BOTH AN INDICTMENT AND A CHALLENGE." Indeed. *Offings and Musings of A. Nutt* came in at a mere 235 pages.

Cyclone Jr.'s book also includes correspondence to and from a banker concerning a $250 loan he sought. He embellishes the banker's replies with poetic flourishes, deeming the institution the "People's Bank" on the "Isle of Pinheads." "Roses Red, Violets Pink; Lend Two-Fifty I Don't Think," begins one note from the banker. Cyclone's reply was sent by "American Express, because Uncle Sam has Leavenworth pretty well filled up already, with bankers."

Both Cyclone volumes were printed by the Courier Press of Sherman with funds raised from prepublication subscribers. Surviving correspondence indicates that a third volume, *Twain Cyclones*, was to be published in the early 1950s. Its author, Agnes Webster, was said to be a descendant of Daniel Webster.

"Beloved friends," wrote Cyclone in a fund-raising letter for the book. "After one year of enjoyable contacts with you great hearts and willing souls, we approach the coveted goal of one thousand protagonizers to hasten the delivery of this great work, representing a lifetime of effort and research by that angelic author."

Cyclone announced that supporters would soon throw a barbecue for the book, and he requested that subscribers send pictures of themselves. "Photographs in hand," he wrote, "are now in a scroll three city blocks long, tied together with Scotch tape. This scroll will be microfilmed and displayed by the side of my picture, already filed with the immortals in the Library of Congress, by movie process to the wide wide world."

In another effort to raise funds for the book's publication, Cyclone ran an ad in the *Dallas Times Herald*, offering a "liberal concession to one hundred Queen Esthers to hang a modern Haman on his own gallows, staging a statewide sales campaign. Glamorous gals of any age, a poignant personality with a yen for showmanship and a genuine sense of humor. Address Cyclone Davis, The Texas Bank Wizard, 339 West Brooklyn, Dallas 8, Texas."

"I am interested in knowing more about your interesting ad," wrote one Miss S. C. Lyons to Cyclone. "Will you please enlighten me?"

"My dear little heart blossom," replied Cyclone. "Your letter of inquiry re. 'my interesting ad' is impressive . . . I'm writing you this letter of authority to sell a famous book by a more famous author, while waiting for you to come from town and satisfy your womanly curiosity. That is one reason why I worded the ad in such an 'interesting' manner . . . I want one hundred or more good looking glamorous gals to sell Miss Agnes' oncoming famous book, to one thousand of my multiplied millions of friends, whose photographs, names, professions, and callings, with my choicest compliments will grace the fly leaves of *Twain Cyclones*, which was to have been the title of a movie, but for the untimely death of my lately illustrious father. P.S. The Haman referred to is the great and powerful *Dallas News*, who for fifteen years has given me THE SILENT TREATMENT."

A copy of *Twain Cyclones* has never been located, and it is still unknown if the volume was ever published. A letter from Cyclone to University of Texas librarians states that he has enclosed two copies of the title, but the stationery makes one wonder if he referred instead to a copy of *Memoir* and a copy of *Offings and Musings of A. Nutt* stacked together as *Twain Cyclones*. The bibliographic mystery endures.

The hospital switchboards were jammed with concerned callers when Cyclone fell ill in 1954. Many recalled the frontier-style campaigner's announcement for the governor's race earlier that year. Cyclone proclaimed, "The National Thinkers Council, 530,000 Friends of the Aged Councils, the Texas Pension Association, the Society of Six Hundred and, of course, the American Brush Club, and some few boneheads have filed their 73-year-old champion protagonist of Tom Paine's Rights of Man for governor of gullible, galloping Texas. Cyclone Davis, the bewhiskered sage of Sulphur Springs, for twenty years a resident of Dallas, and perpetually importuned for thirty years to run for public office, dollar-drafted by every state in the nation, three foreign countries, and the District of Columbia, has of recent years responded to that appeal by running for almost every office under the sun and never been elected to but one."

After losing the race but before the strike of the kidney ailment that untethered his spirit, Cyclone made one final optimistic leap of faith. Perhaps sensing that he neared the end of his earthly journey, he robustly declared his candidacy for the United States presidency, two years ahead of the 1956 election. "How can I lose?" he asked incredulous members of the press. "I'm an international character. I've talked face to face with more people than any other politician who ever lived. Besides that, I'm a freak of nature: I haven't been sick—not even a headache—in over sixty years. People are bound to vote for a healthy politician."

Still, as early as the 1930s, Cyclone reflected on the brevity of this life and the magnitude of eternity. "In the richness of my eventide," begins "A Parting Word and Finis" in *Offings and Musings of A. Nutt*,

> I will want to leave something of my soul behind
> That neither ghoul nor vermin can destroy,
> Nor crumbling marble mark my shrine;
> A word, a thought, a song, a rhyme,
> An act of comprehension
> That man to man or myrmidon may mention.

And the "Finis":

> If you have enjoyed this book please broadcast it, otherwise tie it to your receiver. I already know it's mostly BUNK AND BLARNEY
>
> ADIOS.

3

Port Arthur's Popeye, Bet-a-Million, and the Brownie Man

W hen Port Arthur tycoon John W. "Bet-a-Million" Gates took friends on hunting trips in area marshes in the early twentieth century, the parties' guide was often a young Englishman named Lawrence P. Arnold. In 1908, Arnold, a thirteen-year-old orphan, stowed away on a ship bound for America. After a stormy crossing, he arrived in Port Arthur. "This is it," he announced. "This is where I stay." In 1915, he went to work for the Gulf Oil refinery.

After Arnold had all his teeth pulled around 1930—the year in which Popeye became a national figure—a co-worker told him he resembled the cartoon mariner. Flattered, the Englishman began to mimic the spinach-eating seaman and to call his wife Olive Oyl. Arnold often performed the role to the delight of Port Arthur kiddos at the downtown Kress store, and he was a longtime fixture in parades. The pipe-puffing sailor appeared at the 1936 Texas Centennial celebration in Dallas as "Gulf Oil's own original Popeye." The next year, he was on deck in Crystal City for the unveiling of the Popeye statue in the "spinach capital of the world." He made his final appearance in a Christmas parade in the early 1960s.

The southeast Texas city has seen more than its share of distinctive individuals. Namesake Arthur E. Stilwell wrote that Port Arthur "may not be the only city ever located and built under direction of the spirit world, but it is undoubtedly the only one . . . so recognized and acknowledged." In his 1921 book, *Live and Grow Young*, the visionary railroad and town developer explained that spirits he called "Brownies" advised him in a dream to "locate your [railroad] terminal on the north shore of Sabine Lake . . . And there occurred to me a picture of a city . . . here in this landlocked harbor, safe from the most devastating storms, [where] we could create a port."

In 1899, control of Stilwell's railroad fell into the hands of investor John W. "Bet-a-Million" Gates. The financial titan had already made

"I yam what I yam," proclaimed Port Arthur's Popeye, officiating at all Popeye-related Texas activities, including the dedication of Crystal City's Popeye statue in 1937. Courtesy of W. M. Timmerman Jr.

Texas history in the 1870s when he visited San Antonio on a barbed-wire sales trip and convinced skeptical cattle barons to purchase the newfangled fencing by setting up a demonstration corral on one of the plazas. Gates earned his nickname for wagering hefty stakes on virtually anything—for example, a race between two raindrops on the window of a train.

Gates' biographers wrote that moneyed Easterners who dealt with the barbed wire and steel tycoon perceived him as a "gross, uncouth westerner who ate peas with his knife and whose belch could be heard through the Waldorf's Peacock Alley." Nonetheless, his effective coup in Port Arthur positioned him to reap great riches when oil gushed at nearby Spindletop in 1901.

4

Governor Willie

O il booms attracted some of the most remarkable characters in the country, and every boom had 'em. In the giant East Texas Oil Field, discovered in 1930, the leading performance folk-artist was Henry Ralph Wooley, known throughout the field as "Governor Willie."

"The famous oil field orator," as photographer Jack Nolan described him, was called "Oil Field Willie" when he arrived in Kilgore in 1931, after honing his intense performance style at "all the good booms." Robert M. Hayes, of the *Dallas Morning News* East Texas bureau, wrote that Willie enjoyed "a flamboyant, make-believe career," waging mock political campaigns for state and local offices. "Listeners often were astounded at brilliant flashes of logic that punctuated his speeches," noted Hayes. Others heard fiery tirades about "crooked politicians," delivered mostly in an incomprehensible language of his own invention. Still, as former Kilgore resident Travis Hedge recalled in 1999, the governor's addresses "were worth in entertainment value whatever you could afford to pay him," and his audience often "showered him with coins and even dollar bills."

Another Kilgore citizen described Willie as "the most fantastic per-

WILLIE. THE FAMOUS OIL FIELD ORATOR
HE HAS MADE ALL OF THE GOOD BOOMS
SOME FOLKS THINK AN UNSEEN
POWER GUIDES HIM BUT WILLIE
CLAIMS TO KNOW EVERY THING.
HE CAN DRAW A CROUD OF LISTENERS AT
ANY TIME AND HOLD THEIR ATTENTION.
JACK NOLAN PHOTO

Chief Executive of the East Texas Oil Field, Henry Ralph Wooley, aka Governor Willie, made remarkable speeches on Kilgore street corners and at area political rallies. As photographer Jack Nolan noted, some folks thought "an unseen power" guided Willie. Courtesy of the East Texas Oil Museum, Kilgore.

Governor Willie tries out an "electric chair," perhaps to help promote a film at Kilgore's art deco movie palace, the Crim. Courtesy of the East Texas Oil Museum, Kilgore.

sonage I ever met." Legend has it that many a wildcatter donated to Willie's campaign fund in the hopes that the "court jester of the oil belt" might bring them luck at the well. "Some folks think an unseen power guides him," added Jack Nolan, "but Willie claims to know everything."

As reported in the "Gushings By Gus" column of the *Kilgore Daily News* in 1932, Willie announced his candidacy for Texas governor "on a liberal platform that includes ten-dollars-a-barrel oil, ten-cent beer, cutting officers down to one gun, bigger dance halls, higher skirts, and free roses for women." He also campaigned against government enforcement of proration (the limiting of the amount of oil pumped) by martial law and called for "the removal of all soldiers."

Though he lost the state gubernatorial race to Ma Ferguson, Willie emerged victorious as "Governor of the East Texas Oil Field." In that exalted office, he orated on street corners and at East Texas conventions and held political rallies in Kilgore's art deco movie palace, the Crim. Governor Willie stumped for "more oil wells but less oil, more beef but less beefing, and more rain but less mudslinging." His candidacy, he explained, was "subject to the action of the plutocratic primary." He vowed to "Hiss Hitler, Muzzle Mussolini."

In the 1980s, Kilgore old-timers told writer Ann Ruff that Willie's recorded speeches were more popular on local jukeboxes in the 1930s than Al Dexter's "Pistol Packin' Mama," a nationwide hit inspired by life in an East Texas Oil Field honky-tonk. While no archival audio of Governor Willie has been located, Kilgore historian Terry Stembridge unearthed a silent film of the governor pouring on the political brimstone. As Terry points out, Willie's stump style seems to have perhaps been influenced by newsreels depicting the sharp, emphatic gestures of Benito Mussolini. Willie's clever wordplay reminds one of Will Rogers and Groucho Marx.

Well-heeled sponsors like Mayor L. N. Crim ensured that the governor could chow down at Kilgore cafés and enjoy fresh stogies from the corner drug store. His constituency also pitched in for his printed placards and campaign literature. Oil men provided Willie with suits from Kilgore's finest men's clothier, the Hub. One resident recalled him occasionally sporting a huge sombrero or an old-fashioned Scottish golfing outfit complete with knickers and bonnet. In a 1970s oral history project, Dr. James L. Nichols, history professor at Stephen F. Austin State University, reported seeing the governor wearing "a cowboy pistol and boots" with "some kind of badge" that made him look "like the deputy sheriff."

Reminiscing in 2000, former Kilgore resident Jim Long said that he first beheld Governor Willie speaking at the corner of Main and Commerce in 1932. "At that time, that corner was the de facto hiring hall for oil field workers, roustabouts, and rig builders," said Jim. "A couple of job hunters were standing nearby and after listening a few minutes and not being able to make sense of what Willie was saying, one said to the other, 'Let's go. He's crazy.' At that, Willie turned on him and said, 'I may be crazy, but you don't see me going to work in the rain carrying a tin syrup bucket,'" which were often used as lunch pails in the oil field.

Ten-year-old Jim followed Willie into the Blackstone Café, "where a plate lunch with soup, drink, and dessert was fifty cents." After five minutes had passed and he had not been waited on, the governor demanded and received fifty cents from the cashier, then went elsewhere to eat. "Willie's mental capacity was such that it would earn him a place in the state hospital these days," explained Jim. "But in the early '30s everyone took care of their own."

The governor refused to be intimidated by those of supposedly superior intellect. Dr. Nichols' oral history text includes an oft-told story about the time Colonel Ernest O. Thompson had to leave early from a Kilgore banquet. As head of the Railroad Commission of Texas, the agency in charge of oil regulation, Col. Thompson wielded immense power in the East Texas field. Explaining that he had to fly out to Wichita Falls, the colonel cut his speech short and apologized for his abrupt departure. "Willie was sitting in the front row," said Dr. Nichols, "and knocked them all in the aisles" when he asked the commissioner, "Who the hell invited you here in the first place?"

Col. Thompson might have asked the governor a similar question when, at some point, Willie threw his sombrero into the ring to challenge the commissioner's re-election. "I have the goods on Thompson and will expose the whole thing," the governor told reporters. "There will be plenty of fireworks and not a single fizzle. My minutemen have been busy, and they have a load of information. I have been pledged support of the Blackshirts, blue shirts, and nightshirts." Challenging Thompson to a debate, Willie said the colonel could "choose the joint."

A performance folk-artist with that much bravado naturally, from time to time, ran afoul of the law. In the early days of the East Texas boom, Kilgore police ran Willie in for having no visible means of support. Told that he would have to pay his fine by picking peas at the county farm, the governor snorted, "I didn't plant them peas, I don't eat peas, and so, as shore as hell, I'm not goin' to pick any damn peas!"

"The governor tended to get a little loud when in his cups," added Jim Long, and law officer Ivey Knox "would put him in the cooler until he sobered up." Jim described Ivey as "an overweight six-footer, wearing a wide-brimmed hat and a pearl-handled pistol on a tooled-leather belt . . . I never heard a bad word against him except from Governor Willie." But the lawman came to the governor's rescue in his last campaign in 1940. "He was running for 'public suspecter,'" Jim explained, "a new office [invented by Willie] with duties to be determined chiefly by him and to consist of watching all elected officials closely." Willie's campaign slogan was "No grifters, no grafters, no insects in the rafters."

Jim was standing with Knox at the *Kilgore Daily Herald* election party. "Results for the different areas and contests were posted on a blackboard as they became available," Jim continued. "Governor Willie was on the other side of the group . . . and as the results were posted showing Lightening of Longview outdistancing Willie, the governor became more and more upset. But when the announcer announced that the governor had won because Ivey Knox had recovered Willie's stolen ballots, Willie came rushing over and gave Officer Knox a big hug and pumped his hand."

A bittersweet victory, it was the governor's last campaign. "Kilgore was different yesterday," sighed the *Longview Daily News* on December 3, 1941. "Governor Willie was gone." "He was buried with the pomp and style of a chief executive," noted the *Henderson Daily News*. The 34-year-old governor died as a passenger in a head-on collision "on Highway 26 near the Lacy Refinery." Jim Long identified the site as "the Longview highway, near where Interstate 220 crosses—there were honky-tonks on that corner from about 1936 on." The *Kilgore Daily Herald* counted Ivey Knox among the governor's pallbearers.

"Few men," added the Longview paper, "were better known among the oil fraternity than this court jester of the oil belt, whose antics and homespun humor were as East Texas as the derricks and slush pits he loved."

• • •

The discoverers of the East Texas field, Columbus Marion "Dad" Joiner and A. D. "Doc" Lloyd, are much better-known than the Governor, and are almost as colorful. Dad Joiner was a 70-year-old, Shakespeare-quoting wildcatter who oversold shares in his discovery well in a scenario echoed by the plot of the movie *The Producers*. The Alabama-born Joiner had been a Tennessee state legislator and a once-wealthy Oklahoma landowner before he refined his "nose for oil." His self-taught geologist, the corpulent Doc Lloyd, had worked in an Ohio drugstore and studied medicine before striking out for the gold rushes in Idaho, the Yukon, and Mexico. At some point, he toured the country with Dr. Alonzo Durham's Great Medicine Show, peddling remedies derived from oil. Drilling on Lloyd's advice shortly after World War I, Joiner would have discovered the vast Seminole and Cement fields had he been able to drill deeper.

Because the area around Kilgore, Longview, and Henderson was sandwiched between nonporous layers of limestone and Austin chalk—in a formation new to industry experts called a stratigraphic trap—the major oil companies had passed on the patch of East Texas that, according to Joiner, held "a treasure-trove all the kings of the earth might covet." On a trip to Galveston in 1926, when he was reportedly feeling suicidal over his money woes, the wildcatter had dreamed that he would discover a huge oil field in the rolling hills of Rusk County. After a lengthy search, he found the spot that matched his dream on land belonging to Daisy Bradford. To help raise drilling funds, Doc Lloyd crafted a geological report in which every statement was incorrect, except—amazingly—for one. Doc predicted that Dad would find an "ocean of oil" in the Woodbine sand formation at about 3,500 feet.

And Dad did.

5

Bobcat Carter

Wayfarers to the Big Bend region in the 1930s often beheld white-bearded Henry F. "Bobcat" Carter hopping around in the middle of the road. The performance folk-artist sometimes even blocked traffic so that folks would have to stop, listen to his yarns, and pose with him for snapshots. Dressed in tatters and a crumbling sombrero, Bobcat presented a weathered visage that suggested a strange, long-lost uncle of western actor Gabby Hayes.

"I won't tell where I'm from just because I'm stubborn," Bobcat tittered to the *Alpine Avalanche* in 1935. "The law is always wanting my picture. They think I'm some escaped convict, or escaped from an insane asylum." To one Marathon resident, Bobcat was "that nasty old devil that lived at Persimmon Gap." To many other folks, he was a treasured Big Bend tourist attraction.

Tracking Bobcat in 1972, Sul Ross State University folklorist C. Ross Burns uncovered a passport Carter obtained at Villa Acuña, Coahuila, Mexico, in 1929. The document declared that Carter had begun life in

Missouri in 1843. Interviewing Trans-Pecos residents who'd known the aged desert character before his death in 1940, Burns learned that Bobcat drifted into Texas around 1900 and became known as "Prairie Dog" Carter around San Angelo and Christoval. He had been contracted to poison the animals, and word got around that he consumed them as well. As he told the *Avalanche*, "I've eaten most every kind of varmint there is except skunk. Why not?"

After hunting for a time in Mexico, an 87-year-old Henry F. Carter showed up in Big Bend around 1930. In the *llano despoblado* his trapping and dining habits earned him a new nickname: Bobcat. The last few years of his life, the elderly maverick lived in a tin shed near W. A. Cooper's store at Persimmon Gap. When he got too old to trap, Bobcat sold eggs and chickens from his shed and, at some point, got a twelve-dollars-per-month pension from the county.

To obtain the pension, Carter had to sign a pauper's oath, which took away his right to vote. But on election days, he'd be at the polls in Marathon, pitching such a stink that, as Hallie Stilwell noted, election officials usually gave him a ballot just to end the harangue. Some town residents remembered Bobcat, apparently euphoric over doing his civic duty, performing somersaults and handsprings on Marathon's main street.

As such calisthenic ability at an advanced age indicates, Bobcat—despite his primitive hygiene—enjoyed excellent health. "A man's a fool if he ain't his own doctor at fifty," Bobcat explained to the *Avalanche* in 1935. "I came to this country forty years ago, skin and bone, couldn't lift sixteen pounds of water. I stayed here five years and still my health was bad. Then one day while I was going from Marathon to Ozona I took stock of myself. I decided that God (now here's where folks think I'm crazy) didn't just make all these things, myself included, and then run off and leave it. It's natural to come back and admire your work—just as an artist does. But somehow I wasn't there when he came. It's a trick of the mind. Every fellow has to learn for himself. I dropped sickly thoughts and knew that God would fix me up. Well, laugh or not, He did . . . I haven't spent one nickel for a doctor in thirty-five years."

Two years later, Bobcat put that philosophy into action when he fell ill. Belle Henderson, whose family had boarded Carter for a time at their area ranch, sent him some Christian Science pamphlets that helped him get back on his feet. For the last three years of his life, whenever

Depression-era Big Bend ambassador Bobcat Carter was usually unarmed when he greeted visitors to the *llano despoblado*. Courtesy of the Archives of the Big Bend, Sul Ross State University, Alpine, Texas.

31

beset with a cold or other minor ailment, Bobcat would lie on his cot repeating the mantra "Mind over matter."

Though some regarded Carter as a desert hermit, he was a sociable host at Persimmon Gap. The 1935 *Alpine Avalanche* profile noted that Bobcat always offered guests a drink from his "Wine of Life." The concoction was "made of grapes, peach peelings, apples, a little sotol, and anything else he can find. He drops these in a barrel and lets nature do the work." Some of the bravest visitors sampled his famous bobcat stew. Oftentimes, he'd caterwaul a few lines from a favorite song, such as "The Streets of Laredo."

Bobcat took sick again in the early fall of 1940, entered the Alpine hospital, and died on October 14. His death certificate listed "hypostatic pneumonia, aided by senility." But as folklorist Elton Miles observes in his 1976 book, *Tales of the Big Bend*, "Some believe his death was caused by an enforced violation of his lifestyle. When he arrived at the hospital, they say, the first thing they did was give Bobcat Carter a bath and that is what killed him."

6

William F. Drannan

A Hero, or "Nothing but a Damn Liar"?

As Commodore Hatfield attested, Texans have long assumed a natural right to deviate somewhat from the truth. "Captain" William F. Drannan, who spent his twilight years in the health resort town of Mineral Wells, went so far as to record his revisions of reality in two thick books.

Drannan packed his 1900 tome, *Thirty-one Years on the Plains and in the Mountains*, and his 1910 opus, *Capt. W. F. Drannan—Chief of Scouts*, with hair-raising adventures on the western frontier. The books, which supposedly chronicled his days as a trapper, scout, and Indian fighter with such blue-chip westerners as Kit Carson, Jim Bridger, and General George Crook, found a wide readership, especially among early-

Capt. William F. Drannan died in 1913 in Mineral Wells, where he spent his twilight years selling his books of frontier adventures to spa visitors.

twentieth-century boys eager for exciting tales from the Wild West. (One of the titles was reportedly reprinted one hundred times.) Many bought copies directly from Drannan as he toured the country giving sharpshooting exhibitions.

But readers did wonder. Joe O. Naylor, who later founded the Naylor Company (publisher of a large library of Texana books), bought a copy from Drannan in San Antonio and, like many readers, found himself puzzled when he could find no mention of Drannan in books about Carson and other frontier figures with whom Drannan claimed to have had many thrilling times.

While growing up in Thurber, John S. Spratt read Drannan's books "more than once." In his own book, *Thurber, Texas: The Life and Death of a Company Coal Town*, Spratt recalled once seeing Drannan at the Palo Pinto County Fair, where he wore "fringed buckskins" and had "long, flowing white hair" under "a large Stetson hat." To young Spratt, Drannan "reeked of Indians, buffalo, and beaver."

Eventually, much to the chagrin of Spratt and countless other readers, a "smart-aleck authority on western history" named W. N. Bates busted Drannan's ruse. Bates' 1954 book, *Frontier Legend: Texas Finale of Capt. William F. Drannan, Pseudo Frontier Comrade of Kit Carson* revealed that, in fact, Drannan's wife, Belle, had written the books and that Drannan had, on occasion, fessed up that parts of the books might have been a little "exaggerated." As John Spratt wrote, "It was a terrible blow to learn . . . that my hero was nothing but a damn liar."

Bates wrote that Mineral Wells folks recalled seeing the picturesque figure selling his books on the streets and in the spa's drinking and bathing pavilions. J. W. Goodbar, proprietor of the Crazy Hotel Barber Shop, had read Drannan's books before moving to Mineral Wells and provided shaves for the impoverished elder free of charge. "He would not have his hair cut," reported Goodbar, "and I did not blame him."

When the old scout went home in 1913, the four-foot stone placed at his grave in Mineral Wells' Elmwood Cemetery stated that Drannan had been a Texas Ranger. He had one more tall tale to tell and he did so, eternally, on that headstone.

Or maybe not. Southeast of present-day Prescott, Arizona, a party of archaeologists and historians recently examined a rock carving that read "Killed Indians Here, 1849, Willie Drannan." Though Willie would have been seventeen years old, and traveling through territory previously unexplored by Anglos, the group concluded that the inscription was "probably authentic."

7

Madam Candelaria

"Most Outstanding Female Character of San Antonio History"

Many a San Antonio tourist of the 1880s and '90s, after visiting the Alamo shrine, made their way to a humble abode on South Concho Street or, at other times, to a modest adobe on Laredo Street. There the famed Madam Candelaria received them graciously, a fat Chihuahua at her feet. The passage of time etched deeply into her face, Madam Candelaria seemed older than the great river that ran between Texas and Mexico. Time and again, when strangers or friends appeared at her door, the aged woman performed her dramatic story of surviving the Alamo siege of 1836.

Historians have long disagreed on whether or not Madam Candelaria was actually within the Alamo walls during the battle. Though *The New Handbook of Texas* contends that the majority believe her story, considerable dissent persists. One Alamo-ologist recently labeled another researcher "nuts for giving any serious consideration to Madam Candelaria."

The story generally begins before Santa Anna arrived in San Antonio de Bexar in 1836. Madam Candelaria, operator of a hotel frequented by Texians, received a letter from Sam Houston, asking her to nurse Jim Bowie, who was stricken with typhoid fever. Attending the bedridden Colonel Bowie during the conflagration, she was, according to one of the versions accredited to her, trying to give him a drink of water when Mexican *soldados* rushed in and bayoneted him in her arms.

When William Corner visited her in 1888, as he noted in his 1890 book, *San Antonio de Bexar: A Guide and History*, Madam Candelaria "demonstrated this scene in quite an active fashion," pointing out a scar on her chin caused by the Mexican bayonets. In some tellings, Bowie's nurse also suffered a wound to the arm or hand. Other accounts were markedly different. "She always contended," observed the *San Antonio Express* in her February 11, 1899, obituary, "that James Bowie, the famous scout, died of pneumonia the day before the battle." In that version, Madam Candelaria was shielding Bowie's corpse when *soldados* thrust their bayonets into him, wounding her on the chin and wrist.

Controversy arose concerning the lady's age, as well. Though the 1850 Bexar County census stated that she was forty years old, Madam Candelaria and many others believed that she was much older. In 1885, attempting to settle the issue, family members obtained a copy of her birth certificate or her baptismal records from Mexican archives. Written in the hand of a Catholic priest, the document stated that she was born Andrea Castañón Villanueva in Presidio del Río Grande (between present-day Piedras Negras and Nuevo Laredo) in the year 1785. She confirmed to William Corner in the 1888 interview that she was one hundred years and three months old, though she may have meant 103 years old. "She looked quite the age she said," concluded Corner, "or older, for that matter, great deep ridges, wrinkles and furrows of skin on her face and hands . . . Never suffered any sickness, quite active, alert and quick to perceive and understand. A cigarette smoker. Her eyes, she feared, were beginning to fail her."

The family moved to Laredo when Andrea was three—sometimes she would say she was born in Laredo—and she apparently became a resident of San Antonio in her mid-twenties. Some accounts of her life state that she was present at the 1813 battle of Medina, described by historians as the bloodiest ever fought on Texas soil. Wounds suffered by her first husband in the battle are credited as the source of her enmity against the armies from south of the Rio Grande.

In the mid-1800s, she operated a popular fandango parlor. Longtime San Antonio journalist Charles Merritt Barnes described Madam Candelaria as "the presiding genius" of the fandango in his 1910 book, *Combats and Conquests of Immortal Heroes*. "The fandangos," wrote Barnes, "were held in an old adobe building, a part of which still stands on the west side of Main Plaza at the place afterward known as the old 'Hole in the Wall' restaurant." Another memoirist, Vinton Lee James, anointed Madam Candelaria "the most outstanding female character of San Antonio history." The fandango, James explained in his 1938 book, *Fron-*

Late-nineteenth-century tourists in San Antonio often visited Madam Candelaria to hear her dramatic accounts of the Alamo siege. Several images of
Madam Candelaria show her with a fat Chihuahua, which she felt relieved her
rheumatism. Courtesy of the Daughters of the Republic of Texas Library.

tier and Pioneer Recollections of Early Days in San Antonio and West Texas, "was a relic of former Castilian days . . . where the beaux and belles of San Antonio romped, played, and danced to the sweet strains of the orchestra and dined on the delicious dishes prepared by Señora Cande-laria's own hand."

When Auguste Fretéllière and the painter Theodore Gentilz attended a fandango in the 1840s, the festivities took place near Military Plaza. At the time, the two Frenchmen were awaiting the arrival of Empresario Henri Castro, the namesake of Castroville. Gentilz created a lively painting of the fandango, and Fretéllière left a splendid word-picture of the affair in his memoir, "Adventures of a Castrovillian."

> The sound of the violin drew us to the spot where the *fête* was in full swing. It was a rather large room of an adobe house, earthen floored, lighted by six-tallow candles . . . At the back, a great chimney in which a fire of dry wood served to reheat the *café*, the *tamales* and *enchiladas* . . . A Mexican woman in her forties, with black hair, dark even for her race, bright eyes, [a vision of] extraordinary activity, above all with the most agile of tongues—such was Doña Andrea Cande-laria, patroness of the *fandango*. At the upper end of the room, seated on a chair which had been placed on an empty box, was the music, which was a violin. That violinist had not issued from a conservatory, but on the whole he played in fairly good time. He was called Paulo, and being blind, played from memory. The airs, for the most part Mexican, were new to me. The women were seated on benches placed on each side of the room. The costumes were very simple, dresses of light colored printed calico, with some ribbons. All were brunettes with complexions more or less fair, but generally they had magnificent black eyes which fascinated me. As for the men, they wore [unusually] short jackets, wide-brimmed hats, and nearly all the Mexicans wore silk scarfs, red or blue or green, around their waists. The dance which I liked best was called the quadrille. It is a waltz in four-time with a step crossed on very slow measure. The Mexicans are admirably graceful and supple. When the quadrille is finished, the cav-alier accompanies his partner to the buffet, where they are

served a cup of coffee and cakes. Then he conducts the young lady to her mother or to her chaperon to whom the girl delivers the cakes that she has taken care to reap at the buffet. The mother puts them in her handkerchief, and if the girl is pretty and has not missed a quadrille, the mama carries away an assortment of cakes to last the family more than a week.

Surely, whether her tales of surviving the Alamo battle were true or not, Madam Candelaria developed a love of theatricality and performance during her reign as San Antonio's fandango queen. It isn't clear exactly when that flair for drama inspired her to begin making herself so publicly available as an Alamo survivor, but John S. "Rip" Ford later wrote of having known her as such as early as 1847. For a time, Madam Candelaria may have greeted tourists at the shrine itself. Souvenir cabinet photos depicting the Alamo and Madam Candelaria were available at some point, and by 1882, she had become such a noted tourist attraction that she could have taken her show on the road. "I was offered a fabulous sum to take my mother to the Atlanta Exposition to show her as the only remaining survivor of the battle of the Alamo," her son Santiago told the press after her death in 1899. "It was not the first offer of the kind I had to refuse."

Though she had detractors during her lifetime, such as Alamo survivor Susanna Dickinson, her supporters included not only Rip Ford but other such prominent nineteenth-century Texans as Mary Maverick. In 1889, Ford, who visited Madam Candelaria a number of times, penned a testimonial to Governor Ross in support of a state pension for the aged lady, alluding to her "acts of kindness extended to Texians in the dark hours of revolution." One of her obituaries stated that she had been among the Tejanas "put at hard labor by the Mexican soldiers as punishment" for helping the revolutionists. Legislators awarded her an annual $150 pension in 1891, the same year that the Alamo Monument Association added her name to the list of those present in the Alamo during the battle. Many voices praised her charitable work in 1849, when she assisted stranded pilgrims bound for the California gold fields, and later, when she nursed victims of the smallpox epidemics of the 1860s and '70s.

"She was quite anxious to remember everything," wrote Rip Ford in his memoirs. "With reference to a man whom many regard to be an imposter, and of whom no one has ever gleaned anything authentic, Señora Candelaria said she could endorse him as another child of the Alamo. She remembered his frightened condition during the bombardment. He clutched her dress as children do, trying to hide his face."

Sage Ford also realized that one must "make many allowances" for the recollections of a person who might be over one hundred years old: "So long and active a life as hers must be crowded—more—overcrowded, and jumbled with the multitude of things to remember."

Describing one of her thousands of performances of the death of Bowie, a *San Antonio Express* reporter noted, in 1892, that Madam Candelaria "made numerous expressive gesticulations, swaying her body to and fro in a highly dramatic style." Detailing her family's genetic good fortune to the scribbler, the possible centenarian "stated that she was never sick in her life and never took a particle of medicine of any kind. She has never even so much as had a touch of headache. Her father lived to the extreme age of 130 years and her mother 120 years."

Though blind for the last few years of her life, Madam Candelaria still enjoyed regaling visitors with the searing drama of 1836. Bowie's illness and death formed the heart of her repertoire, but she often spoke of Davy Crockett as well, recalling "lots of singing, story telling, and some drinking" at her hotel after his arrival and before the arrival of the Mexican army. "Crockett played the fiddle, and he played it well, if I am a judge of music," she continued, drawing a curious portrait of the Tennessean and his demise. Her version may or may not be true, but it differs from the account of his surrender and execution in the de la Peña diary—the controversial document that alleges that Crockett and a handful of other Texians surrendered and were executed by the Mexican army—which also may or may not be true. "He was one of the strangest men I ever saw," Candelaria recalled of Crockett.

> He had the face of a woman, and his manner that of a girl. I could never regard him as a hero until I saw him die. He looked grand and terrible, standing at the front door and fighting a whole column of Mexican infantry. He had fired his last shot, and had no time to reload. The cannon balls had knocked away the sand bags, and the infantry was passing

through the breach. Crockett stood there, swinging something over his head. The place was full of smoke, and I could not tell whether he was using a gun or a sword. A heap of dead was piled at his feet, and the Mexicans were lunging at him with bayonets, but he would not retreat an inch. Poor Bowie could see it all, but could not raise himself from the cot. Crockett fell and the Mexicans poured into the Alamo.

8
___

Three Rode For Texas

"When we want to say it is all up with some fellow," quoth one mother's son in 1884, "we just say G.T.T." Across the country, many an ornery hombre had "Gone To Texas." Three of the most notorious—Billy the Kid, Jesse James, and John Wilkes Booth—were not only wanted desperadoes who headed to the big state to hide from the law. According to history, they were also dead.

The problem with history, of course, is that it happened a long time ago. Books say that Old West lawman Pat Garrett punched the Kid's ticket to purgatory in New Mexico in 1881. Jesse got it in the back a year later up in Missouri. And a federal posse saw to it that Booth kicked the bucket in Virginia soon after assassinating President Lincoln in 1865.

In the 1870s, however, an eccentric, Shakespeare-quoting bartender fell ill in Granbury, Texas. Certain he would die, the miserable cuss confessed to lawyer Finis Bates that he was actually John Wilkes Booth. And early in 1950, two elderly Texans in western duds, J. Frank Dalton and Ollie "Brushy Bill" Roberts, appeared on the NBC radio program *We the People*. Dalton informed the nation that he was Jesse James, still living at 102 (or thereabouts), and Brushy Bill—either on that broadcast or months later—fessed up to bein' the 90-year-old Kid. Let's track these performance folk-artist sons of guns and their legends of life after death in the Lone Star State.

Long believed to have departed the planet, "Jesse James," "Billy the Kid," and "John Wilkes Booth" showed up in Texas. Illustration by and courtesy of Jimmy Longacre.

JESSE

At least three well-seasoned gentlemen ended their days in Texas with folks thinkin' they mighta been Jesse. When banker and former Brownwood mayor Henry Ford died around 1910, rumor pegged him as the bank-robbing Missourian. More recently, Betty Dorsett Duke of Liberty Hill staked her family claim to bad-boy fame. "For as long as I can remember," says Betty, "I've heard that my great-grandfather, known in Texas as James L. Courtney, was really the outlaw Jesse James."

Betty cites family tales of Grandpa's fortune in silver dollars and gold bars, cached at his farm near Blevins. "When riders arrived after dark," she adds, "Grandpa would blow out the coal-oil lantern and lie down across the doorway with his pistol cocked." Betty also points to similarities in photos of Grandpa and his family to images long accepted as depicting the James clan.

After her book, *Jesse James Lived and Died in Texas*, appeared in 1998, Betty heard from Willie Ford, a grand-nephew of Bob Ford—the man that history records as Jesse's killer. The book, Willie wrote, affirmed a story he'd heard all his life. But still unconvinced, Betty's kinfolk blocked her effort in 1999 to have Courtney's body exhumed for DNA testing.

A year later, in a fitting addition to the saga of perhaps the most famous Jesse James impersonator, J. Frank Dalton, believers tried to exhume his mortal husk in Granbury, but they unearthed the wrong remains. Both the Courtney and Dalton camps discount a 1995 test that confirmed Jesse is buried in Missouri. Such voodoo science woulda given J. Frank a hissy fit. "I don't give a hoot whether anybody doubts I am Jesse James," he barked at a Chicago reporter in 1948. "I am—and that's that!"

With his long white hair and frontier outfits, Dalton was "a familiar character" to East Texas oilfield folks for many years. Self-penned stories of his Civil War exploits with Quantrill's Raiders and other adventures appeared in papers like the *Troup Banner* as early as 1932.

The *Lawton Constitution* of Lawton, Oklahoma, broke the story of Dalton's ascension to Jessehood in 1948, convinced of the aged outlaw's identity by "ironclad evidence." In Guthrie, Oklahoma, a 108-year-old former slave named John Trammel, who reportedly cooked for the James Gang, swore that J. Frank was Jesse in the flesh. Jesse James biog-

When J. Frank Dalton/Jesse visited Al Jennings in California in 1948, the two elderly desperadoes "gossiped like housewives over a back fence." Courtesy *San Francisco Examiner*.

rapher Homer Croy, who visited while Dalton was "curing a bile attack with whiskey and donuts," didn't buy it. But, like old-time wanted posters, the headlines jumped from town to town. Basking in the limelight and tipsy on publicity, the antique desperado went on tour. According to the *San Francisco Examiner*, Dalton/Jesse and fellow outlaw Al Jennings, 85, staged a duel in a San Leandro, California, Fourth of July parade and later "gossiped like housewives over a back fence."

"Boys," Al crowed to the *Oakland Tribune*, "there ain't a bit of doubt on earth. This here is Jesse James!"

When Dalton/Jesse hit the Windy City, one Virginia Marmaduke reviewed his performance folk-art for the *Chicago Sun-Times*. "The watery-eyed old man showed a flash of genuine Missouri hillbilly ire when it was suggested he might be a fake and was in Chicago to grind some special ax," wrote Virginia. In town to see a doctor about his hip, Dalton/Jesse lay in a hospital bed "in a swank suite at the Parkway Hotel, Lincoln Park West," Marmaduke reported, noting that the scene seemed as though it had been arranged by a "Hollywood press agent." Surrounded by flowers, Dalton/Jesse "wore a Buffalo Bill beard and hair dress . . . Orvus Howk, who described himself as an oil and cattleman from Centerville, Texas, and a distant relative of the star of this drama, met guests at the door." There was even a press kit of sorts, with photos of Jesse, brother Frank, and ma Zerelda. Dalton/Jesse said they'd probably wander out to Montana and "take in some state fairs along the way."

Late that year, 1948, the state of Texas took Dalton off the Confederate pension rolls, suspending his monthly hundred-dollar check because he'd been out of the state for six months. The following August, Wick Fowler reported in the *Dallas Morning News* that the comptroller would reinstate the payments if he'd quit being Jesse James. "I can make a lot more in a month being Jesse," J. Frank retorted, "than I got being Frank Dalton."

While such statements might seem to contradict the notion that Dalton truly believed that he was Jesse, I would argue that there was plenty of room in J. Frank's psyche for competing motives and views of reality. Even though he enjoyed the extra income and living high on the hog while on tour, Dalton's performance as Jesse was inspired by much more complex issues than a simple craving for cash.

In January 1950, Dalton/Jesse received the press in a Big Apple hotel bedroom. His two sidekicks that evening, according to a report in the *Austin American-Statesman*, were "two witnesses, Brushy Bill Roberts, 90, who claims to have been a member of the James Gang, and Colonel James R. Davis, 100, who says he was a U.S. Marshal for the Cherokee Indian nation." (It's possible that the paper got the description of Brushy Bill's claimed identity wrong, but it's also possible that Roberts was claiming to have been a member of the James Gang before he began claiming to be Billy the Kid.)

That same month, Dalton/Jesse unsuccessfully petitioned the circuit court of Franklin County, Missouri, to officially restore to him "my Christian name of Jesse Woodson James . . . under which I entered this world and under which I wish to leave."

Whoever the colorful old gentleman was, he headed off into the sunset in the searing heat of August 1951. He spent the last week of his life in a small house in Granbury, its porch festooned with his press clippings and signs that invited folks to meet "the real Jesse James" for a small donation.

Days after his death, a Chicago press agent named Rudy Turilli, representing a tourist-attraction cave that Jesse James used in his Missouri stick-up days, offered ten thousand dollars to anyone who could prove that J. Frank Dalton was not the real Jesse. And interest continued, even as the Old West receded further into the past. A 1962 report in *Climax* magazine quoted one Jesse Lee James of Manitou Springs, Colorado declaring that his late grandfather, J. Frank Dalton, was in fact Jesse James. The magazine's reporter interviewed nurses who had cared for Dalton in a Longview hospital in 1947, the year before he emerged as Jesse. "He wouldn't let us take his boots off the whole time he was here," recalled nurse Varna Southerland. "When we started to remove them, he rebelled and said that he had killed men for a hell of a lot less than that."

Carl Breihan analyzed what he called Dalton's "carefully fabricated claims . . . submerged in a morass of confused and contradictory self-revelations" in an article titled "The Last Pretender" for *Frontier Times* magazine. In 1979, Betty MacNabb mused in the *Marble Falls Highlander* about the "mysterious, tall bearded stranger" who "lived at the old Roper Hotel in Marble Falls some thirty-five years ago." As late as 1992, treasure-seekers were digging for a safe that Dalton/Jesse had supposedly buried in Waco back in 1918. Then in 2000, after years of increasing interest in his story, Dalton-was-Jesse believers tried to dig up the outlaw himself.

Though they unearthed the wrong body, perhaps some of those present at the Granbury cemetery might have been convinced of Dalton's claimed identity by reading the characteristically purplish account of his death in the January 1952 issue of *Police Gazette*:

> The searing Texas heat converted the tiny room into a scorching oven, but the frail, white-haired man shivered . . . Hoarse whispers clawed their way out of his throat in the rasping rattle which precedes death. It was August 15, 1951, and the old man who had lived 104 years was dying . . . But his steel-blue eyes still glittered unafraid and for the last time, through thin, almost bloodless lips, the old man sneered at those who questioned his identity. "I am Jesse James."

BILLY

" J ust a few months after the death of Billy the Kid, in a dark room at old Fort Sumner," wrote Virgil N. Lott and Mercurio Martinez in their 1953 book, *The Kingdom of Zapata*, "there appeared on a ranch in the north end of Zapata County a slender youth with buck teeth and hands like a woman." For months, the stranger worked on the ranch, then disappeared. Later, folks learned he was . . . the Kid.

In 1932, the *Mentone Monitor* broke the story that Billy lived near El Paso and described him as "a white-haired old man, who plays a fiddle at country dances and acts queer, no longer fearing the law but fearing vengeance of friends of those he killed."

Six years later, the *El Paso Times* noted that Major Gordon W. "Pawnee Bill" Lillie and other members of the National Frontiersmen's Association were searching for the living Kid. According to a memoir scribbled by one Brushy Bill Roberts in his old age, Pawnee Bill knew that the Kid survived past 1881. Brushy Bill's robust résumé included a stint with Pawnee Bill's Wild West Show in the 1890s. Under names like Rattlesnake Bill and the Texas Kid, Brushy wrote, he also performed in the saddle with Buffalo Bill and Booger Red.

Brushy Bill cowboyed on Tom Waggoner's spread at Decatur, lost two ranches to revolutionary turmoil in "Old Mexico," rode with Teddy's Rough Riders in Cuba, hung out with outlaw queen Belle Starr, and worked as a plainclothes officer in Gladewater during the wild East Texas oil boom, to name just a few of his alleged exploits as a "living dead man."

Brushy Bill showed up in Guthrie, Oklahoma, in July 1948 to testify to the press that J. Frank Dalton was Jesse James. "I've known him for seventy-eight years, and [I've known] for all this time that J. Frank Dalton was Jesse James," swore Brushy Bill, described in the article as an "82-year-old former scout and Indian fighter." Brushy Bill went on to explain that his own father, Al "Wild Henry" Roberts, was on hand to identify the body when Bob Ford shot Charlie Bigelow, and Wild Henry agreed to fib that the body was Jesse James.

The spirit of Billy the Kid—or a performance folk-art interpretation of that spirit—seems to have invaded Brushy Bill's heart and mind, body and soul sometime in 1950, either during or after returning from the

trip to New York to appear on nationwide radio with Dalton/Jesse. That
April, Severo Gallegos later told the *El Paso Times*, his old amigo Billy
the Kid visited him in a Ruidoso, New Mexico, tourist court. "I've seen
William H. Bonney [a pseudonym adopted by Billy, whose given name
was Henry McCarty] more times than you can count," said Gallegos.
And in July, the Kid contender visited his old friend Martile Abel, 89, in
El Paso. "He is alive," Mrs. Abel told the *El Paso Herald Post* in November. "Others have tried to impersonate him, but the man I talked to in
July was the real Billy."

In the East Texas village of Cayuga, 95-year-old Jim Watts, who had
been a member of the posse that trapped the Kid in 1881, backed up the
generally accepted historical version. "I even played poker with him and
drank with him . . . saw him quite frequently." Testifying that it was
indeed the Kid who had been shot by Garrett, Watts added, "He looked
awfully dead to me."

In late November, Brushy/Billy appeared in Santa Fe, New Mexico,
with his attorney, William Morrison, to request a pardon for his ancient
misdeeds. Unconvinced that Brushy was Billy, Governor Thomas
Mabry refused.

A month later, Brushy Bill Roberts died on the streets of Hico,
where his own legend soon took root. Computerized photo analysis
and other high-tech investigations have proven and disproven—
depending on your interpretation—that Brushy Bill and the historically
accepted Kid were two different dudes.

"There's not another like him in Texas," wrote reporter Thomas
Turner when Brushy died, "a straight-eyed, fast-talking little man who
spun a wondrous tale. And it was a fascinating yarn. Some of it could be
verified. Around Hico, the folks sort of poked fun at his fabulous stories
. . . But the beauty of it was that the part of his endless tale that was
true was enough. Brushy led a life that a Hollywood horse-opera writer
would have discarded as too unbelievable."

BOOTH

General Albert Pike was bending his elbow in the bar of Fort Worth's
Pickwick Hotel with Sam Houston's son Temple Houston and
other gents one day around 1885 when he suddenly turned pale. "My
God—" stammered the general, "[that's] John Wilkes Booth!"

COPY-RIGHTED
FEBRUARY 16 1898
By F.L. Bates

John St. Helen/Booth as he appeared in Finis Bates' 1907 tome, *Escape and Suicide of John Wilkes Booth*. Courtesy of the Center for American History, the University of Texas at Austin, CN06905.

The visage that startled Pike appeared in Texas in the late 1860s or early 1870s. Calling himself John St. Helen, the mysterious stranger settled in the scenic Paluxy River village of Glen Rose. In a riverside log cabin, he sold whiskey, tobacco, and other staples to locals and folks camped near the town mill.

Area pioneers later recalled St. Helen's "polished manner and cultivated bearing." The "center of attraction" at community gatherings, he recited English poetry and drama with "eloquence" and had a captivating "stage presence." At the same time, he evinced a "restless and haunted, worried expression," as "flashes from his keen, penetrating black eyes spoke of desperation and capacity for crime."

When a federal marshal arrived in Glen Rose to wed a local gal, St. Helen vanished. Around 1872, he appeared in nearby Granbury, where he worked as a bartender. After knocking on Hades' door, near death, and "confessing" to lawyer Finis Bates, he recovered and disappeared again. Some believe he taught school in Bandera under the name William J. Ryan. The late Concho County attorney E. H. Swaim—who spent years researching Booth's Texas saga—was convinced Ryan had also lived and taught in Eden.

In 1903, in Enid, Oklahoma, a house painter called David E. George confessed that he was Booth as poison coursed through his bloodstream. "I desire to see the curtain of death fall upon the last tragic act of mine," orated George/Ryan/St. Helen/Booth to three Enid ladies, according to Finis Bates' 1907 tome, *The Escape and Suicide of John Wilkes Booth*. "I killed the best man that ever lived."

An Enid undertaker mummified the body, and Bates took "John" on a book-promotion tour. In 1920, the "Carnival King of the Southwest," William Evans, obtained the gruesome curio and likewise took the body on the circuit. Old-timers who viewed the mummy when John was returned temporarily to Glen Rose agreed that he was the man they'd known as St. Helen and who could well have been Abe's assassin. Mrs. P. L. Embree recognized the man she had once danced with, by the Paluxy so long ago.

Evans retired to Declo, Idaho, and posted a sign outside his farmhouse: "See The Man Who Murdered Lincoln." In 1932, John Harkin, a former sideshow tattooed man, bought the mummy for five thousand dollars but failed to turn a profit until 1937 when he hooked up with the Jay Gould Million-Dollar Show. The following year, a *Saturday*

Evening Post story marveled that "America's leading mummy" had been "bought and sold, leased, held under bond, kidnapped, and seized for debt."

Though most historians have agreed with Lincoln assassination expert James O. Hall that there "are enough John Wilkes Booths around to float a battleship," at this late date, John St. Helen is still a wanted man: a recent message posted on the Internet by a forensic pathologist, hoping to run DNA tests, requests information on his whereabouts.

• • •

Were any of these men who rode for Texas actually Jesse James, Billy the Kid, or John Wilkes Booth? If I knew the answer to that, I'd have my own 1-900-PSYCHIC-TV commercial. We may never know for sure, but their legends will intrigue us for generations to come. Though she mentions only one of the aforementioned mavericks, Mary Daggett Lake's assertion in a 1931 *Fort Worth Star-Telegram* article rings true for all three men: "The myth that is weaving itself about the life of John Wilkes Booth bids fair to rival that of Paul Bunyan, Alkali Ike, and Pecos Bill . . . if, indeed, it is a myth."

9

Wild Bill's Final Performance

A similar myth grew around the outlaw legacy of one Wild Bill Longley, who had a date with the gallows in Giddings in 1878. At some point, folks began speculating that Wild Bill had paid off the sheriff and survived the necktie party. Some believed he lit out for Louisiana, where he lived another forty-one years as the "mystery man of Iberville Parish." In 1987, Giddings flea-market owner Woodrow Wilson, whose grandfather had married Wild Bill's sister, executed a work of performance folk-art about the family legend. The 67-year-old Wilson "hung" himself to prove that a properly-equipped condemned man could survive his own hanging. Outfitted with a harness similar to mountain-climbing gear—and similar to the rig he believed his ancestor used to fool the noose—Wilson suffered a few cuts and rope burns when he

A descendant of outlaw Wild Bill Longley, Woodrow Wilson had himself "hung" in Giddings in 1987 to prove that a properly-harnessed condemned man could survive his own necktie party. Courtesy of the Associated Press.

dropped eight feet on the homemade gallows. "I'm alive," he hollered to the crowd of one hundred, who broke into cheers. "I did it the way Bill Longley did."

Though few of the onlookers were local folks, Wilson hoped the event might inspire an annual Bill Longley Days festival, similar to the success of Frontier Days in Round Rock where thousands witness the repeated reenactment of the shoot-out death of outlaw Sam Bass. "Sam Bass was no meaner than Bill Longley was," Wilson complained to the press. "In fact, Bill Longley was meaner. He killed more people. I don't see why Giddings can't have something like that."

The town may someday embrace the notion, but it won't be because Wild Bill survived the gallows. DNA testing proved in 2001 that the body in Longley's grave was that of Wild Bill himself.

10

Sain-toh-oodie Goombi and Two Braids Tommy

Many of the more complex Old West identity performances involved children captured by Indians. Millie Durkin (also written as Durgin, Durgan, and Durkan) was taken captive by Kiowas at eighteen months of age in the Elm Creek Raid, near Fort Belknap, in 1864. In 1930, several Fort Belknap-area old-timers helped Mrs. Sain-toh-oodie Goombi, then in her sixties, reach the conclusion that she was the same Millie Durkin. The blue-eyed, light-haired Mrs. Goombi had grown up with Kiowas in Oklahoma.

Sain-toh-oodie and her family attended pioneer reunions in the Belknap area until her death in 1934. The visits always created a sensation in the newspapers and helped salve ancestral wounds between cultures. Young County native Barbara A. Neal Ledbetter sat in the Newcastle High auditorium as a grade-schooler, watching Mrs. Goombi speak Kiowa on the stage as her grandchildren performed Indian dances. The experience set Barbara wondering, and half a century later, in her 1982 book, *Fort Belknap Frontier Saga*, she concluded that the real Millie Durkin had died shortly after her capture, advancing the alternative theory that Mrs. Goombi had been kidnapped near Mason. Other researchers have disagreed, and exploration of the mystery continues today on the Internet.

An even more confounding captive performance is the saga of Tommy "Two Braids" Stringfield. In an 1870 attack in McMullen County known as the Stringfield Massacre, Indians (most accounts say it was Apaches) killed both Stringfield parents and one son. Tommy's sister Ida, though left for dead, survived, and four-year-old Tommy was taken captive. According to the tale spun in the 1911 book, *Captured by the Apaches*, purportedly written by Tommy "Two Braids" Stringfield, the young captive grew up "riding with those wild spirits" and rubbing shoulders with the likes of Geronimo and Quanah Parker. In 1909, a dying Apache named Death Face, the story goes, informed Two Braids of his true identity.

Many believed that Mrs. Sain-toh-oodie Goombi was Millie Durkin who had
been kidnapped by Kiowas near Fort Belknap in 1864. Courtesy of Old West
Photos.

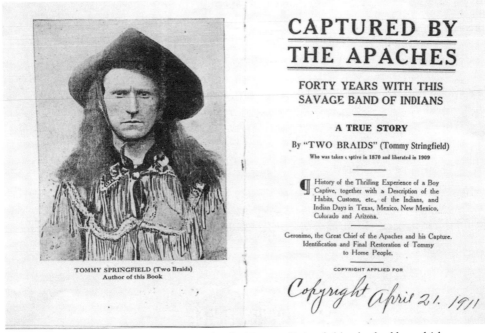

CAPTURED BY
THE APACHES

FORTY YEARS WITH THIS
SAVAGE BAND OF INDIANS

A TRUE STORY

By "TWO BRAIDS" (Tommy Stringfield)
Who was taken captive in 1870 and liberated in 1909

History of the Thrilling Experience of a Boy Captive, together with a Description of the Habits, Customs, etc., of the Indians, and Indian Days in Texas, Mexico, New Mexico, Colorado and Arizona.

Geronimo, the Great Chief of the Apaches and his Capture. Identification and Final Restoration of Tommy to Home People.

COPYRIGHT APPLIED FOR

Copyright April 21. 1911

TOMMY SPRINGFIELD (Two Braids)
Author of this Book

Showman Ora Woodman claimed to be Tommy Stringfield, who had been kidnapped by Apaches as a child and was renamed Two Braids.

Two Braids traveled to San Antonio, where he was reunited with sister Ida. Skeptical at first, Ida eventually became convinced that the "bronze-faced man who wore his hair in two strange-looking braids" was indeed her long-lost sibling and hosted Two Braids and his daughter Nucki at her family's home in Medina for several months. Other kinfolk and family friends also reportedly confirmed identifying marks they'd seen on four-year-old Tommy before the attack.

Upon learning that his parents' burial site in McMullen County lacked a marker, Two Braids and Nucki began touring South Texas giving exhibitions of Indian horsemanship and trick riding to raise the necessary funds. "This was quite an undertaking, as I was without a dollar and did not understand the ways of the Texas people," wrote Two Braids. The *Eagle Pass News-Guide* reported that "his feats were very clever," and that his life would make "refreshing reading" if more facts were known.

Meanwhile, Ida grew suspicious and began searching for more facts, soon learning that the stranger who claimed to be her brother was in reality a Wild West showman from Oklahoma named Ora A. Woodman. Ora, according to the 1906 book *History of Oklahoma and the Oklahoma Territory* by J. L. and Ellen Puckett, heard the story of the Stringfield Massacre that same year and assumed the Tommy "Two Braids" Stringfield identity. A flyer for a performance in Carlsbad, Texas, in the summer of 1906 advertised a trick riding performance by the "Famous Character," Two Braids, and Nucki, "a half-breed Apache . . . the only one of her tribe now on exhibition." In the 1930s, Ora Woodman settled in Roswell, New Mexico, where he continued his identity performance by adopting a new handle, Uncle Kit Carson, claiming to be the nephew of the famous scout.

I I

Hondo Crouch

"Imagineer"

Willie Nelson, of course, reigns as the preeminent early-twenty-first century Texas maverick. As he's aged, the Red Headed Stranger has weathered into a beloved combination of Walt Whitman and Gabby Hayes, set to quintessential American music. John Russell "Hondo" Crouch, though he left this world in 1976 at the young age of sixty, was a similarly complex and lovable figure. As John Goodspeed put it in the *San Antonio Express-News*, Hondo was "a cloning of Will Rogers, Peter Pan, and a white-haired country sage."

John Russell Crouch observed in his diary that he was "different" while growing up in the town of Hondo, located between San Antonio and Del Rio. As an All-American swimmer at the University of Texas, he was dubbed the "Hondo Wonder." Shortened to "Hondo," the name stuck, and it was a perfect handle for a man whose maverick nature beheld this life as an extended performance to be frolicked through as naturally as the act of breathing. Even at age twenty-three, working as a counselor and swimming coach at Camp Rio Vista on the Guadalupe River, Hondo was described as "a character out of a story book."

Luckenbach artist-in-residence Hondo Crouch erased almost any trace of the separation of art and life. Photo by Jim Steely, courtesy of the Texas Department of Transportation.

For decades, he ranched near Fredericksburg, raising cattle, sheep, and goats. His bride, Helen Ruth, also known as "Shatzie," was the daughter of Adolf Stieler, crowned "Goat King of the World" by *Life* magazine and the American Sheep and Goat Raisers in 1945. In the 1960s, Hondo led a theatre troupe that performed in Grapetown, Waring, Comfort, and other Hill Country spots. The Crazy Comfort Bunch, as the group was sometimes called, was so original and creative that they drew audiences from Houston and Dallas. Several seasons began with the "premiere" of *Blank Dank*, a homemade film by Rex Foster in which Hondo played all seven roles. When the *Saturday Evening Post* profiled him as a "colorful character" of LBJ Country in 1966, curiosity seekers from beyond the state began finding their way to his caliche ranch road. Rubberneckers who managed to meet Hondo invariably returned home with a souvenir dose of his gentle yet wicked ribbing.

In her 1979 book, *Hondo, My Father*, Becky Crouch Patterson described him as "a mystery, a frustrating puzzle." Once, when the family pleaded with its patriarch to make clearer demarcations between his serious side and his relentless joshing, Hondo retorted, "You can tell I'm not teasing when my lips aren't moving."

But she also notes that Hondo's children were "steeped in his magic," which included a fascination with and reverence for even the smallest creations of the natural world. Hill Country rambles in Hondo's ancient pickup truck took on a mystical wonderment Becky described as "pasture worship."

From 1963 to 1975, vaguely disguised as Peter Cedarstacker, Hondo wrote a column called "Cedar Creek Clippings" for the *Comfort News*. The six hundred columns satirized life in the mythic town of Cedar Creek and beyond. "The band was all Gutowsky and played Porkchopsky's Chopstixsky Concerto in B Flatsky," he wrote of a fictional Gutowsky Reunion. "There was gobs of food and . . . 72 different kinds of potato salad . . . The main topic of conversation wasn't when Joe stuck a cedar limb through his body while breakin' a wild horse, or when Uncle Udo died in an ant nest. They talked 'bout more terrible things, like the time a Gutowsky nearly missed a meal!"

The legend of Hondo Crouch grew even more exotically maverick-esque in 1971, when he bought the tiny town of Luckenbach (approximate population: four). That fall, the miniburg hosted the first Susan B. Anthony Memorial Chili Cook-Off, a playful taunt to other such contests that barred female contestants. "For the next five years," Becky wrote, Hondo was "a sought-after personality . . . the star attraction at Texas folklife festivals and fairs . . . People loved his weathered looks, his faded cowboy garb. His twinkly blue eyes, pixielike youthfulness, and keen wit captivated all who saw and heard him." His guitar playing and soulful singing of cowboy and Mexican songs enchanted audiences as well.

When a journalist asked his plans for the town, Hondo replied, "Nuthin'. We're gonna have dances and eventually a place to eat, and we're thinkin' of even having a restroom, although that's still in the planning stages."

Hondo installed a lone parking meter in his town, and a mailbox on a twenty-foot cedar pole stood ready to receive air mail. Old-time patent medicines and other goods still filled the town's country store, along with a sign boosting "Ma Ferguson For Governor of Texas." A new sign went up above the store's doorway that read, "Oldest store in continuous operation I know of, I think—Moses, 1849."

The rural municipality proved a perfect vehicle for "a hobo cowboy whose stage was any street corner or oat field," as Becky Crouch Patterson described her father. In the summer of 1973 Mayor Crouch wore a black wig, top hat, and buffalo robe for the first Luckenbach Great World's Fair. Some ten thousand people showed up for the hurrah, which included old-time crafts, *charro* performances, Kiowa dancers, and contests in musket shooting, tobacco spitting, chicken flying, cow-chip throwing, and armadillo races. "Freaks, straights, rednecks, businessmen, the whole spectrum of humanity was represented," Becky recalled.

Over fifty thousand attended the Non-Buy Centennial celebration at Luckenbach in 1976. "Bad Taste Awards" were given out all day long for the most crass exploitation of the nation's two-hundredth birthday. An antique cannon was fired, and Hondo awarded Purple Hearts to folks who fell down in the grass. He invited the Prince of Wales and Elizabeth Taylor to the shindig, but they appear to have stayed home. If Liz and the prince had attended, though, Hondo would have treated them just like everyone else. "Everybody is somebody in Luckenbach," he philosophized. Hondo was often uncomfortable, though, when such hordes overran the miniature metropolis. When folks asked directions to the town, he usually allowed that it was "between Corpus Christi and Dallas."

As the "Clown Prince of Luckenbach" became more and more celebrated, Hondo could have printed money with his maverick charisma. But he preferred to stay home mostly, whittling and keeping an eye on his town. "I never get on a stage," he liked to say. "The stage just seems to get under me." He did appear on the national television program *To Tell The Truth* as the humorist owner of a tiny Texas town, but he reportedly turned down offers to be on *Hee Haw* and to be featured in a Carnegie Hall performance with Jerry Jeff Walker. When he died of a heart attack in September 1976, he was booked to appear on *The Tonight Show with Johnny Carson* and had a film performance in *Pony Express Rider* in the can.

Hondo obscured the separation between art and life so completely that even some of his greatest admirers felt he overdid it. "He would always act as if he was just an old tobacco chewin' country boy that don't know nothin', but he was actually very intelligent and well-informed," said fellow raconteur John Henry Faulk. "He took the character he played seriously—too seriously, I always felt, because he never stepped out of character. It became real to him."

A month before Hondo died, Bob Hope appeared at a benefit for the Nimitz Hotel in Fredericksburg. Hondo strode out on stage in the middle of Hope's monologue and handed him a note that read, "Your fly is open." Then, as Hope dabbed at his tears of laughter, Hondo, representing the Luckenbach Chamber of Commerce, presented the famous comedian with an ax handle in lieu of a golf club. "Sorry it doesn't have a head on it. You see, it's hard to get a head in Luckenbach.

"I really enjoyed your little bit on the show," Bob Hope later wrote to Hondo, "and I hope to get down there and take a look at your town. It must be something if all the natives are like you; it must be the first town with a net under it!" Enclosing some glasses with "Thanks For The Memories" printed on them, Hope continued, "I hope you will think of me when you drink and smoke whatever you smoke—it could be your suspenders! . . . Stay well and happy and keep that sense of humor."

12

Trek Stars

Hickey, Hoopie, Plennie L. Wingo, and Others

PLENNIE L. WINGO

In 1931, Abilene restaurateur Plennie L. Wingo (1895–1993) got the idea of a lifetime while chatting with some teenagers about the unusual stunts people were pulling to grab publicity and make money during the Depression. Having had to close his restaurant and go to work for $12 a week, Wingo understood why folks were resorting to dramatic gestures. The youths figured it had all been done: flagpole-sitting, pushing a peanut up Pikes Peak with one's nose, Lindbergh's flight across the Atlantic, and so on. Suddenly, Wingo found these words coming out of his mouth: "Well, boys, not everything has been done. I don't believe anyone has ever walked around the world backwards." A half-century later, Plennie explained the logic behind his sudden inspiration in his autobiography, *Around the World Backwards*. "With the whole world going backwards," he wrote, "maybe the only way to see it was to turn around."

Obsessed with the idea, Wingo became a performance folk-artist. He first secured unexpected approval and enthusiasm for the idea from his wife and daughter. Then he undertook a rigorous training regimen with a chiropractor who advertised that he could train anyone to accomplish any physical task. "He said it was a fantastic notion," Wingo recalled. "He'd never heard of such a thing. He felt it was against nature and didn't even know if it was possible. But he was game to help me."

Wingo bought special glasses with rearview mirrors that were used by motorcyclists and sports car racers. He figured the reverse trek would pay off by selling cards along the way and hiring his backwards walking out for advertising stunts. Shoe companies were reluctant to sign on as sponsors, but the Southwestern Exposition and Fat Stock Show in Fort Worth kicked in two hundred and fifty dollars for ten days of backwards-walking publicity. "I made my first public appearance," Wingo wrote, "dressed

61

Plennie L. Wingo sold postcards along the way to help finance his backwards walk around the world. Courtesy of the Ken Wilson Postcard Collection.

in cowboy clothes, boots, and ten-gallon hat, advertising the Fort Worth Stock Show." Though he was nervous at first, Wingo's training came in handy, and he maneuvered streets and sidewalks handily.

The backwards walker wore a suit when he headed east from Fort Worth in 1931. His locomotion was aided by a beautiful cane "made of coffee wood carved with mystic symbols and a buffalo horn handle." When Wingo hit Dallas, the mayor granted him special permission to wear a sign (in violation of the city's sign ordinance) on his back reading "Around The World Backwards."

As he backed across the country, newspaper headlines greeted him coming and going. "REACHES ST. LOUIS ON FREAK JOURNEY," announced the *St. Louis Post-Dispatch*. "Hiker, Traveling in Reverse, Keeps Up with Schedule on Weird Journey Around Globe," reported the *Evening Star* of Washington, D.C., noting that it took Wingo only fourteen days to go from St. Louis to Chicago and that he sometimes averaged twenty miles a day. The *Star* also ran a political cartoon that featured a drawing of Wingo under the words "News Bulletin—Man From Texas Starts To Walk Around The World Backwards." A Republican elephant-man and a Democrat donkey-man stand looking at the drawing as one says to the other, "That's nothing new! We've both got lots of chaps been doing that for years."

After Wingo ceremoniously backed down the gangplank before crossing the ocean, citizens on the European continent found him just as intriguing, though the paper in Budapest welcomed him as a "Crazy Texan." Things went along swimmingly until he arrived in Istanbul, where his unusual quest got him thrown in the pokey for several days. Eventually, though he was unable to walk backwards completely around the world, he made it to California by boat and put himself in reverse to trek back to Texas.

In the eighteen months since he had set out, Plennie L. Wingo had earned a lifetime of experience, and he reprised his transportation performance decades later. To celebrate the nation's Bicentennial in 1976, he walked backwards from San Francisco to Santa Monica and appeared on *The Tonight Show with Johnny Carson*. The reverse pedestrian is also one of only three Texans mentioned in Dr. David Weeks' and Jamie James' 1995 book, *Eccentrics: A Study of Sanity and Strangeness* (the other two are Howard Hughes and James "Silver Dollar" West). Weeks and

James note that Wingo's "world record" for walking backwards was later bested by Marvin Staples, a Chippewa Indian from Minnesota.

As Wingo approached Mineral Wells on his trek home in 1932, an elderly man who had taken the waters in the resort city advised, "You take a few of them baths, and you will be able to turn around and walk forwards good as ever."

HICKEY

Ed Hickey, the "Hitch-Hiking Cowboy from Texas U," trekked the nation from 1929 to 1933, collecting autographs on ten-gallon hats. According to his 1939 travelogue, *Hickey's Th' Name*, some 47 governors, 433 U.S. congressmen, 96 senators, 200 Olympic athletes, myriad movie stars, and other celebrities signed Hickey's hats.

"Glorifying the Texas Ten Gallon Hat," as the University of Texas student newspaper described his heady undertaking, Hickey purchased his first ten-gallon for $3.98, then began his signature quest from the Alamo in 1929 with thirteen cents in his pocket. After a brief stop in Austin, where Governor Dan Moody signed the chapeau, it was easy hitching and signing until he reached Washington, D.C. There, every member of President Herbert Hoover's cabinet signed the hat, but Hoover himself refused, suspicious that Hickey had some "ulterior motive."

Nonetheless, back home, the *San Antonio Light* ran a photo of Hickey on the White House steps with a caption that reported, "HICKEY ENTERS THE WHITE HOUSE. LOCAL BOY MAKES GOOD." Hickey rushed in, the paper joshed, "where Democrats and Angels feared to tread." The story noted that when the collector met the president, he blurted, "Herb, Hickey's the name. How about your autograph?"

When Hickey finessed and pestered his way into a meeting with Franklin Delano Roosevelt, then serving as governor of New York, FDR asked him, "Hickey, where's your horse?" Roosevelt further opined that the Hickey hat act was a "million-dollar idea." Explaining that the press had been hounding him to find out when he'd sign the hat, the governor of Massachusetts asked Hickey cheerfully, "Where the hell have you been?" The mayor of Boston weighed in that the project was a good way to keep folks' minds off the Depression.

Admiral Byrd exclaimed, "So, you're the fellow from Texas with the famous autographed sombrero." New York City mayor Jimmie Walker

Hickey posed on the White House steps, minutes before meeting Herbert Hoover and unsuccessfully attempting to add the president's autograph to his hat. Courtesy of the *San Antonio Light* Collection, Institute of Texan Cultures.

weighed in with "Hello there, Texas." Al Smith gifted Hickey with one of his trademark Brown Derby hats, and Tom Mix presented him with a $250 sombrero. Back in Texas for a pit stop, Will Rogers teased Hickey when he asked for Rogers' autograph but had no pen, which Hickey had also done to Huey Long previously. Hickey was so excited to get the autograph of John Nance "Cactus Jack" Garner that he fell into a patch of prickly pear. In his San Antonio hotel room, Sir Harry Lauder modeled the ten-gallon hat while wearing his traditional kilt.

The two-for-the-price-of-one governors, Ma and Pa Ferguson, signed Hickey's hat, as did Governor Alfalfa Bill of Oklahoma. Hickey's heart leapt when he received a telegram stating that Hoover had reconsidered and would autograph the hat, but when the Texan reached the White House, the president said he had changed his mind and refused again.

On and on it went, all across the country. By 1944, when New York journalist Joseph Allen ran across a Hickey ad in Big Apple papers, Hickey had been working as a machinist in the Brooklyn Navy Yard for three years. In the booklet *Hickey, the "Cowboy Caruso,"* Allen explained that Hickey's Texas friends had nicknamed him the Cowboy Caruso as a joke. "Everybody used to kid him about his voice because he couldn't sing cowboy songs and he couldn't sing opera—but he loved the 'Star-Spangled Banner,' 'The Road to Mandalay,' and the 'Song of the Vagabonds.'" The ad that drew Allen's attention proclaimed: "Hickey, the 'Cowboy Caruso' from Texas—vocalizes F above high C a hundred times in 1 hour daily fortissimo—before practicing the semi-classics. Cynics—Critics—Promoters—and Sponsors—WELCOME."

Hickey explained to the newsman that his voice had once been on its way to becoming "a big, booming baritone," but after a few singing lessons, "it started to go up and up." He placed the ads in New York papers, "hoping that someone would help him bring his voice back down to earth."

HOOPIE

Harm Bates "Hoopie" Williams of Texas City became a trek star in 1929 when a friend dared him to roll a hoop from Texas City to New York City. Harm named his hoop Irma for "a certain girl in Texas." Made of steel, Irma was forty-eight inches around with an inch-wide tread, and Harm rolled her along with a bamboo pole with a steel crossbar—spec-

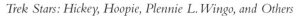

Ralph Sanders set out from the Rio Grande Valley for New York City in May 1930 riding a bull named Jerry.

ifications that met the requirements of the International Association of Hoop Rollers. Losing fifteen pounds and a lot of shoe leather, Hoopie and Irma rolled into the Big Apple six months after leaving Texas City.

WHETHER BY DONKEY, GOAT, OR BULL

One May day in 1930, Ralph Sanders of San Benito swung into a saddle that was strapped on a large, black bull named Jerry. "From the Lower Rio Grande Valley to New York City," read a placard Sanders held on his chest for the press. Ralph figured the bull ride would take about nine months at ten miles per day. Ben Stack of Harlingen, scheduled to follow him a few weeks later in a cart pulled by a donkey and a goat, reckoned he would reach New York before Ralph and Jerry. Both men sought to outdo Bill Williams of Rio Hondo, who, as the *San Antonio Light* reported, "lost an election bet and rolled a peanut from that city to Harlingen, and then gained renown by using his proboscis to roll the peanut up Pikes Peak."

13
_____

Arizona Bill

In the opening decades of the twentieth century, other trek stars traveled the land telling tales—both true and "improved"—of the wild old days in the West. Many a kid treasured the memory of meeting a grizzled yet gentlemanly frontier army veteran named Raymond Hatfield Gardner, better known as Arizona Bill. Riding his beloved burro, Tipperary, the trek star looked like a visitation from the past with his Wild-West-Show locks and face full of whiskers.

Arizona Bill seems to have spent much of the last six years of his long and eventful life at Fort Sam Houston in San Antonio. He died in the Alamo City in 1940 at the age of ninety-four, but thanks to the efforts of another veteran, George Miller, Arizona Bill's saga after his death is almost as intriguing as his life.

Miller met Arizona Bill in 1939 at the army hospital at Fort Benjamin Harrison, Indiana, where Miller was serving as an x-ray technician. Laid up as a patient there for two weeks, Arizona Bill regaled Miller with his dramatic narratives and displayed fraying documents that attested to his tales. "One letter," retired Master Sergeant Miller wrote to the Director of Cemetery Services for the Veterans Administration in 1976, "was a letter of commendation from General U. S. Grant commending Gardner for his service as courier for the general . . . The second letter was from Mrs. Elizabeth B. Custer, thanking him for services to General Custer as a scout."

Miller, in 1976, was nearing the end of a long journey to prove that Raymond Hatfield Gardner had indeed served his country. Remembering that Arizona Bill, upon leaving the Fort Benjamin Harrison hospital, had invited the x-ray technician to visit him in "my city," retired

The peripatetic Arizona Bill spent his twilight years at Fort Sam Houston in San Antonio.

Master Sergeant Miller moved to San Antonio in 1950. When he learned that Gardner had been buried in an unmarked grave at San Fernando Cemetery #2, instead of at Fort Sam Houston, because the army couldn't locate Gardner's service records, Miller began his quarter-century curatorial quest. After the VA finally located the old scout's enlistment papers, in dusty cavalry archives, Gardner was reburied with full military honors in Fort Sam Houston National Cemetery, on Veterans Day in 1976.

Like Miller, a number of folks who attended Arizona Bill's funerals had heard his stories 'round a campfire (or hospital bed). In the 1930s, many more listened to Arizona Bill's numerous appearances on San Antonio radio. Others had read about his adventures in magazines and newspapers. Most versions generally agree that Arizona Bill said that he was born in 1845 in Louisiana. When his father was stricken with gold fever, the family headed west in a covered wagon. Somewhere in the Texas Panhandle, the toddler Raymond Hatfield Gardner was captured by Comanches. Traded to the Sioux some years later, the story goes, the red-headed boy didn't know he wasn't an Indian until he rejoined his own culture around the age of thirteen, perhaps rescued by soldiers, or, as in one account, by escaping to a white settlement in East Texas.

When the Civil War broke out, the teenager joined the Union Army, reenlisting several times after the war. He became a scout, reportedly serving as a valued translator for Generals Crook and Miles—who are said to have renamed him Arizona Bill—during their hunt for Geronimo in the land of Gila monsters and giant saguaros. Of his service with Custer, Arizona Bill said he was lucky and missed out on the Battle of the Little Bighorn. He also tried his hand at mule trading, prospecting, and riding for the Pony Express.

And like anybody who was anybody in the Old West, he is said to have performed with Buffalo Bill. An affidavit in the files of the Fort Sam Houston Museum testifies to Arizona Bill's "Wild West" participation. "When I was a child in 1912," swore Max W. Link Sr. in San Antonio on July 18, 1977, "I was attending school at Louisville, Colorado, when Buffalo Bill brought his Wild West Show to town . . . Annie Oakley and Arizona Bill were two of the many entertainers with the show."

After enlisting in the army, Link was stationed at Fort Sam Houston in the 1930s, where he ran into Arizona Bill. "We talked about the Buffalo Bill performance at the Louisville school," testified Link, "and about Buffalo Bill who had passed away in 1917." According to various chronologies, Arizona Bill joined the Cody troupe in the mid-1880s or early 1890s and traveled the world with the show until shortly before it closed for good in 1913. In the Roaring Twenties, Arizona Bill reportedly lived for a time in Montana, where he assembled a small buffalo herd with the aim of taking to the road with a trained buffalo act.

Perhaps finding bison difficult to train, Arizona Bill shed the wooly beasts and acquired some burros, then set out on his Old West celebrity tour. And like all such picturesque figures, he was buoyantly observed by the press wherever he and his burros rambled. In early 1926, for instance, the *Arizona Daily Star* noted that Arizona Bill was passing through Bisbee, on his way to the Sesquicentennial celebration at Philadelphia. He told the *Star* that he had lived in Arizona, apparently off and on, since 1865.

In 1927, passing through Little Rock, Arkansas, Arizona Bill camped near the home of Gerald J. McIntosh. "Bill wore a scout's uniform," McIntosh recalled in a 1965 *Frontier Times* article, "consisting of a short-sleeved khaki shirt with an open neck, khaki trousers with leather leggin's, brogan shoes, and a campaign hat." Arizona Bill showed the young Gerald a letter of reference said to have been signed by General Nelson A. Miles, Buffalo Bill Cody, Captain Jack Crawford (the Poet Scout), and other western icons. When the old scout and his burros moved on, Arizona Bill astonished his young Little Rock friend by presenting him with the letter. "The letter is very difficult to read," McIntosh wrote in 1965, "and I have never been able to satisfy myself that I can make it out correctly."

Today, the letter rests in the archival sanctity of the National Cowboy and Western Heritage Museum in Oklahoma City, as part of the Gerald J. McIntosh Western Ephemera Collection. Museum cataloging describes the "document of uncertain provenance" as "intriguing and problematic." Dated December 14, 1877, and written in Montana Territory, the paper, according to the finding aid, "purports to be a letter of recommendation for Gardner written by Gen. Nelson A. Miles . . . which mentions his service in the 'Nez Perce Raid & Campaign.'"

When Arizona Bill passed through Burnet, Texas, in the spring of 1929, the *Burnet Bulletin* described him as "perhaps the last noted Indian scout of the great West." The paper reported that Bill camped in the city park with his three burros—Tipperary, plus Dynamite and Salome—and planned to deliver a lecture to the local Boy Scouts.

By most accounts, the 88-year-old trek star parked his wandering spirit at Fort Sam Houston in 1934, where he preferred sleeping in the stables with Tipperary to indoor slumber in a bed. He told the *San Antonio Light* that year that he credited his longevity to "abstinence from liquor, tobacco, and matrimony." In a letter to *Western Story* magazine in

1936, Arizona Bill wrote that he'd been reading the publication for years because it helped to "keep the blues away." When the Ringling Brothers Circus came to San Antonio in 1937, a friend took Arizona Bill to meet actor and showman Tim McCoy, who ran the Wild West Show portion of the circus. McCoy hired the 92-year-old, and Arizona Bill went briefly back on the road before labor trouble caused the circus to fold early in the season. "I talked to the old scout after he came back to Fort Sam," wrote the friend, "and he was all broken up over it."

Arizona Bill's greatest concern as he neared the end of this life in early 1940 was for the welfare of his beloved Tipperary. Military restrictions required that the burro be removed from a Fort Sam Houston corral, but Tipperary found a home with donkeys in Brackenridge Park. "But he is considered an aristocratic donkey," noted Thomas J. Jenkins in a *Frontier Times* story, "and it costs ten cents to ride him, while it only costs five cents to ride any of the others."

The esteem accorded his faithful friend might have eased Arizona Bill's transition to the realm beyond and softened his disappointment at the skepticism some fellow mortals showed to his tales of the wild old West. At his 1976 reburial, retired Master Sergeant George Miller recalled that sometimes, unrolling one story after another, Arizona Bill would "get this faraway look in his eyes and say, 'But nobody believes me.'"

14

Bicycle Annie

Other trek stars covered just as much ground as Hickey, Hoopie, and Plennie, but confined their transportation performances to one locale. Generations of Austinites beheld with awe the enigmatic lady known as Bicycle Annie.

Born Zelma O'Riley in Oklahoma in 1897, she moved to Fort Worth at some point and then to Austin in the late 1930s. "It's the capital, and I wanted to observe what goes on," she allowed in 1964, in one of a handful of cryptic interviews given through the years. In the 1940s she published a small newspaper, *Up and Down the Drag*, which carried small-townish odds and ends, along with snippets about Native American rights. The latter earned Zelma her first nickname, the Indian Princess.

"AMERICAN INDIAN ANNOUNCES CANDIDACY," read the headline of a front-page story in *Up and Down the Drag* on November 25, 1947. Beneath a photo of O'Riley, the brief write-up stated that the "Editor, Publisher, and Owner" of the paper was entering the 1948 race to become the first female president of the United States. "She believes it will take a woman to save America," the announcement continued, "and will conduct her campaign on the preparedness plank."

Most remember the Indian Princess presidential candidate, however, for her perpetual motion. At first—perhaps as early as the 1940s—she rode a bicycle, constantly on the move from one end of town to the other. In time, it seemed that she began to carry her worldly belongings in bags and baskets hanging all over the bike. Folks began referring to her as Bicycle Annie, though the origin of the "Annie" part is unclear.

In time, as she aged and riding the bike became difficult, she pushed the bag-laden bike as she walked along. Two falls in which she broke a hip caused her to switch to crutches and sometimes a walker. Still, she perambulated all about town, becoming famous for heaping abuse on anyone who sought to give her a hand. My girlfriend once got the legendary cussing-out when she tried to help an unsteady, elderly Bicycle Annie across a street. The poet Albert Huffstickler paid tribute to her mysterious omnipresence in verse, and musician Lonnie Mack recorded a song about her.

Bicycle Annie legends and rumors abounded. Some said she was secretly wealthy and owned property all over town. Others said a husband and children had died tragically in the 1940s. Due to her continuous presence on the streets, many assumed she was homeless. But the scant historical record mentions her residing at different apartments and homes. When Austin History Center librarian Biruta Kearl conducted an oral history interview with O'Riley in April 1991, just weeks before she died, Bicycle Annie was living in the Bluebonnet Courts on Guadalupe Street.

Contrary to the hostility of her street persona, Zelma received Kearl warmly and spoke openly about her life. She stated that she had attended law school for a time in order to learn how to better fight for

Native Americans' rights. Her grandfather, O'Riley told Kearl, was Colonel George Hawkins, once the leader of the Choctaw Nation, and his picture hung in the capitol in Washington, D.C. She was writing a book on the subject. "I like to travel and like to be out and be active too, but if you're gonna write a book, you have to stay in," Zelma O'Riley explained. "I'm interested in everything."

15

Moses Evans

"Wild Man of the Woods"

In days gone by, most every spot on the map was home to a mysterious, picturesque figure who dwelled out in the hills, deep in a thicket, or holed up in a cave or a hut at some lonesome bend of a river. In early Washington-on-the-Brazos, it was one Moses Evans, who proclaimed himself the "Wild Man of the Woods."

Born in Kentucky in 1812, Evans arrived in Texas before the revolution and served in the army unit that guarded an encampment of sick Texians and equipment during the Battle of San Jacinto. The service provided him with 960 acres of Texas sod, and though Moses could not read or write (his legal mark has lately been offered for sale at ephemera shows), his efforts in the land business had amassed a sizable estate at the time of his death in 1853.

Advertising himself as the "Wild Man of the Woods" in the *Texas State Gazette* and other early papers, Moses located and surveyed tracts on the frontier in return for a percentage of the land. "He may be found, when not in the woods, at Washington," directed the ad, "where communications will receive prompt attention."

In the 1875 publication, *A Texas Scrap-Book*, Swante Palm described Evans as "a robust, strong frontier character." Palm recalled that "Mose" had "a large sunburnt face, all in flames," with "fiery red hair and long beard." And though Moses, "a man of peculiar looks" and mannerisms, lived and worked in the Austin colony wilds, he enjoyed visiting the settlements, especially during social events at which he sought the attention of colony women, whom he reportedly referred to as "Mister-Ladies."

Dr. J. W. Lockhart wrote about one such occasion in the *Galveston Daily News.* "Away back in the thirties," recalled Dr. Lockhart, "a wedding [and dance] came off in the old town of Washington." As was his custom for all such festive celebrations, the Wild Man of the Woods donned his "highly prized" rattlesnake skin vest. Unfortunately, on that day Moses had "neglected to give this article the necessary airing out which he should have done to preserve its purity and sweetness." Thus, the treasured garment reeked with "a decidedly snakish smell."

To avoid impending social disaster, Moses visited the office of Dr. T. J. Heard for "perfumery" to mask the offensive odor of *Crotalus atrox.* Promising the Wild Man that ladies would be able to "smell you from afar off," Dr. Heard, apparently something of a practical joker, doused Moses' scalp with cinnamon oil. "Moses recovered his head with his immense Mexican sombrero and proceeded on his way to the ball with much self-satisfaction." There, the Wild Man exercised his expertise "in the mysteries of cutting the pigeon wing, knocking the backstep and coming down on the double shuffle," and with a matronly partner soon became "lost in the mazes of the old Virginia reel." Until, that is, the cinnamon oil heated up his scalp so effectively that Moses "ingloriously fled to find cooler quarters."

More pioneer hijinx were perpetrated at the Wild Man's expense in 1850, when settlers began noticing that small amounts of food were disappearing from their homes. Finding small footprints leading into the forest, folks began to speak of the "Wild Woman of the Navidad." The stealthy nibbler was eventually found to be an escaped male slave, but not before a series of elaborate poems had appeared in Texas newspapers, allegedly written by Moses to his "dear Forestina," and in return, by the Wild Woman to "my Wild Man." One of the latter concluded thusly:

> I'm weary, my darling, of being alone;
> Come take the *Wild Woman*, and make her your own,
> Like the dove from the ark, her heart longs for rest,
> And would gladly repose on your *Rattlesnake Vest*.

16

Robert Hall

Sharp-dressed Frontiersman

With a name that sounds like a men's haberdashery, frontier fighter Robert Hall developed a distinctive fashion sense. That eye for style once drove him on a two-hundred-mile round-trip through Indian country to buy his wife Polly a new dress. Living in Cotulla in the 1870s, he sewed himself a fabulous "frontiersman's suit," adorned with the hide, fur, claws, rattles, tails, and horns of most every kind of beast that prowled Texas and Mexico. He wore the outfit at veterans' reunions until his death in 1899.

The *St. Louis Globe-Democrat* described Hall's appearance at a reunion in 1898: "Perhaps the most widely known and most highly respected of all the old Texas veterans is Col. Robert Hall of Cotulla, Texas . . . If he should appear on the streets of St. Louis or at one of the leading hotels dressed in his magnificent frontiersman's suit, it would require more than one policeman to keep the astounded public from crushing him, unless the old veteran took a notion that he did not need the services of a metropolitan police officer . . . The old warrior is 6-feet-4-inches high and 85 years of age. He walks with a firm step, carrying his head erect, and when he appears on the streets of San Antonio or at some other gathering of veterans wearing his extraordinary suit, he is always the observed of all observers."

Hall came to Texas in the spring of 1836 from Tennessee, where—though underage—he'd voted for Davy Crockett for U.S. Congress. Arriving after the Battle of San Jacinto, he joined the Army of the Republic, married Mary Minerva "Polly" King and settled in Gonzales County. As a member of Matthew Caldwell's Ranger company, he helped lay out the town of Seguin in 1838. Two years later, he was wounded fighting Comanches at the Battle of Plum Creek.

When the matter of annexing Texas came up, Hall opposed it, voting, as he later wrote, "first, last, and all the time for the Lone Star." Nonetheless, he joined General Zachary Taylor's army to defend U.S. interests in the Mexican War. (A sword he plucked from the bloody field

Robert Hall's fantastic frontiersman's suit was a hit at veterans reunions in the late nineteenth century. Courtesy of the Institute of Texan Cultures.

at the 1847 Battle of Buena Vista can be seen at the Los Nogales Museum in Seguin.) Hall also opposed slavery and Texas secession, but he still fought for the Confederacy in that "fratricidal struggle."

Hall wore the eye-catching "frontiersman's suit" for the cover of his 1898 biography, *Life of Robert Hall*, written by someone known only as "Brazos." In 1936, the garment was exhibited at the Texas Centennial Exposition, where film star Gary Cooper donned it for photographers.

17

Anthony Banning Norton

"Full-blown Eccentric"

According to the 1983 book *Lone Stars and State Gazettes: Texas Newspapers Before the Civil War* by Marilyn McAdams Sibley, journalist and politician Anthony Banning Norton (1821–1893) earned the distinction of "full-blown eccentric." A Walt Whitman look-alike, Norton may be seen as a star attraction of a maverick subcategory we might think of as hair performance. The *Encyclopedia of the New West* (1881) explains that in 1844, while still living in his native Ohio, Norton was "twitted . . . with the remark that until his beard were grown he had better remain in Jericho . . . whereupon, under the momentary impulse, he vowed that his hair should never be shorn nor his beard shaven until Henry Clay should be president of the United States."

Converting from the Whig party to the Know-Nothings, a much hairier Norton headed for Texas in 1855. The following year, when the abolitionist Norton squared off with the pro-slavery Colonel L. T. Wigfall in a "political tournament" in Marshall, the *Texas Republican* took note of his "long, flowing beard, rivaling in extent, the pictures of the ancient prophets." The paper's editor, Robert W. Loughery, added sarcastically, "He was a most marvelous personage; a second Daniel that was to bring Democracy to judgment, or a David whose mission it was to destroy the Goliath, Democracy, and restore the sinking fortunes of Know Nothingism."

Elected to the Texas legislature as a representative from Henderson and Kaufman counties in 1857 and 1859, Norton stood with Sam Houston and a minority of Texans against secession from the Union. When he became editor of the Austin paper titled the *Southern Intelligencer* in 1859, Norton wrote that he would hold true to his beliefs, "the world, the flesh, and the devil to the contrary." In 1860, he nominated Sam Houston for president at the convention of the Constitutional Union party in Baltimore. There, journalist Murat Halstead described Norton as "a hairy delegate" with "a beard half a yard long, who was dressed in home-spun and bore a great buckhorn-handle cane."

As war amongst the American states began to seem inevitable, personal insults exchanged between Norton and John Marshall, editor of the Austin-based *Texas State Gazette*, became so heated that Norton accepted Marshall's challenge to a duel. Dueling was illegal in Texas, however, so the two agreed to pace, turn, and fire two hundred miles north of the Red River at "Tah-la-qua"—Tahlequah, Oklahoma. Traveling separately, the duelers failed to meet. After returning to Austin, each editor accused the other of dishonor by shirking his gentlemanly responsibility to meet an accepted challenge.

Like most staunch Unionists, Norton had to leave Texas during the war. He returned to Ohio, where he visited and assisted prisoners of war from Texas, acts that won him admiration by the population of his adopted state. Still, sometimes tensions ran high after he returned to the state at the war's end. According to *The Encyclopedia of the New West*, Norton resettled first at Jefferson. There, he published the *Union Intelligencer* "until it was destroyed by a mob, and he was compelled to leave, and ensconced himself in the thickets of Van Zandt."

Moving to Dallas, where he reestablished *Norton's Union Intelligencer*, the shaggy-haired editor was appointed a district judge. Yet despite the fact that the *Dallas News* described him as "one of the most picturesque figures on the streets of Dallas," Norton lost races for Congress in 1866 and 1871, and contests for governor in 1878 and 1884.

"My body was born sometime before the war," Norton told his children late in life, when they asked his age. "But my heart is that of the generation that has grown to manhood since Appomattox."

18

O. L. Nelms

The Most Thankful Millionaire

I remember seeing mysterious messages emblazoned on the Dallas landscape of the late 1950s and '60s: THANKS TO ALL OF YOU FOR HELPING O. L. NELMS MAKE ANOTHER MILLION! And I recall an anxious state of wondering. Who is this O. L. Nelms? How did he make another million? And why is he thanking me for it?

Like most residents, however, I think I finally just took the millionaire's graffiti for granted. Placed on dozens of billboards and tractor-trailers all over the city, the Texas-size thank-you notes probably struck most people as an appropriate symbol for the herd of native wheeler-dealer businessmen that roamed the landscape growing money on mesquite trees. But none, observes Dallas historian Jack Allday, could match O. L.'s "combination of business skills, over-the-top eccentricity, and flair for self-promotion." For sure, nobody had more fun with his dough than Nelms.

The fun started for Ocie Lee Nelms in the East Texas hamlet of Lone Pine, near Palestine, where the family moved not long after his 1907 birth in Cleburne. The future millionaire got his first taste of mercantilism selling hominy door-to-door, straight from the bucket. Noting the youngster's bargaining skills, O. L.'s parents began sending him to town twice a week to sell their farm products, helping out his cowboy-share-cropper father who struggled to keep the family of six going on $20 a month. Soon the boy was upping prices and keeping a neat commission for himself. "That's how I got my first shotgun," Nelms later stated. On the side, he sold possum pelts at 25 cents per possum: "I'd catch 'em and skin 'em on the spot."

Ocie first hit the big city in 1923, breaking into Dallas retail with his own unique approach. The young businessman had special pockets sewn inside his coat and loaded them with fountain pens, combs, cigarette lighters, candy bars, and other goods that busy workers might need during a business day. Bringing his service straight to the public, O. L. would visit downtown Dallas offices, open his coat to display his wares,

In the 1950s and '60s, the thankful O. L. Nelms placed these messages on billboards and tractor-trailers all over Dallas. *Dallas Morning News* real estate editor Steve Brown described the signs as "a forerunner of the current branding craze" in 2003. Courtesy of the *Dallas Morning News*.

and rake in the cash. On several occasions the walking convenience store was run in by the police for questioning. Not only did he prove the operation legit—he racked up healthy sales among the men in blue.

After the Depression hit, Nelms dug up a cache of eighteen silver dollars he'd buried for a rainy day, purchased an old Chevrolet panel truck, and opened his wholesale business. A warehouse soon became his base of operations. The Nelms lived in one part of the building and worked in the other part eighteen hours a day. With a well-thumbed copy of Napoleon Hill's *Think and Grow Rich* in hand, O. L. zeroed in on pursuit of the mythic seven figures, handing out cigars with wrappers that said, "Help O. L. Nelms Make A Million Dollars."

A lot of people must have been smoking those cigars. By the time Nelms sold the business in 1946, the company was reportedly netting as much as eighteen million dollars a year.

Though O. L. dropped his fancy western duds for suits and bow ties in the 1950s, he continued to sport a modest amount of fancy jewelry. Courtesy of Robert Harris with a muchas gracias to Jack Allday.

As his business prospered, Nelms instinctively knew the importance of keeping up an image, and his attire in the 1940s fit the Hollywood conception of a Texas millionaire. Photographs from a 1945 *Saturday Evening Post* article entitled "The Texas Trader" show him decked out in cowboy get-ups flashy enough to satisfy a Porter Wagoner fan. And lest folks take him for a rhinestone wrangler, the Trader sported diamonds on his belt and fingers and a diamond horseshoe stickpin. Even Yankees found him a spectacular sight. Once, when he boarded a homebound train in New York City, passengers in the club car applauded and cheered O. L. as he entered in glittery western duds. "That was kind of pleasant," he told the *Saturday Evening Post*.

After the war Nelms shifted his business activities to real estate, acquiring as many as eight hundred properties that he leased to concerns as varied as warehouses, motels, bars, residences, drag strips, dance halls, and grocery stores. His Dallas shopping center developments included Southern Oaks, Cedar Crest, Stevens Park, Highland Park, and Pleasant Grove. In 1950 Nelms teamed up with the King of Western Swing to open Bob Wills' Ranch House at Corinth and Industrial. A prototype for Fort Worth's Billy Bob's, the cavernous honky-tonk featured a bar inlaid with 1,700 silver dollars and a stall for the famous fiddler's horse, Punkin. Wills even had the horse fitted with special rubber shoes for riding on the dance floor. Two years later the club was sold to the enigma that launched a thousand conspiracy theories, burlesque impresario Jack Ruby. At some point, the name was changed to the Longhorn Ballroom, and eventually the venue's offerings expanded beyond C&W to include acts like the Sex Pistols and 2 Live Crew.

Though Nelms dropped the western garb in the 1950s in favor of conservative suits and bow ties, his unconventional style continued to flourish. Like many of his fellow eccentric Texas millionaires, O. L. seems to have had a thing for silver dollars. Perhaps in an effort to out do the fabled exploits of Houston's Jim "Silver Dollar" West (who liked to fling the eight-bit chips and watch folks scramble for them), Nelms once attempted to round up a million silver dollars.

Figuring the people of Texas needed to behold such a sight, the Most Thankful Millionaire hoped to exhibit the mass of cartwheels at the state fair. The Federal Reserves and printing mints the would-be curator contacted kept passing him on to the next government agency until O. L. found himself talking to the Assistant Secretary of the Treasury in Washington, D.C., Nelms was told that he was welcome to the silver as long as he showed up with a cashier's check for a million dollars and several eighteen-wheelers to transport the thirty tons of gleaming dinero. Furthermore, the Treasury Department would require that the dollars be transported in quarter-inch-thick steel boxes, welded shut and welded to the trucks. Finally, when he figured in the armed guards and insurance and interest lost on the million while it was on exhibition, Nelms discovered that it would cost him $2,500 for each day the money was on display. Fairgoers lost the chance to marvel at a million silver dollars.

Throughout his business and thanking career, Ocie L. Nelms felt that the key to success lay not only in hard work but in an enthusiastic attitude and the cultivation of friends. And the popular businessman proved his theory even in the face of serious illness. In 1970, he developed kidney cancer and underwent an operation at Baylor Hospital. After recovering, the thankful Nelms threw a punch-and-cookies celebration for 150 friends, associates, representatives of Dallas Baptist College, and members of the press. After a color slide show featuring his x-rays, operation, and scenes of the hospital, O. L. presented the college with 125 acres of land valued at half a million dollars.

Two years later, Nelms entered a hospital in Snyder. Shortly before he died there in May 1972, a reporter asked him what had been the most important things in his life. Never one to beat around the bush, he replied, "I've always liked pretty girls, good whiskey, and lots of money."

But the Texas Trader would probably like to be remembered most as the thankful millionaire who never lost touch with regular folks, never forgot where he came from. When he first got rich, the story goes, Nelms would occasionally dress up like a hobo, hitchhike out of Dallas with less than a dime in his pocket, and travel cross-country working odd jobs and collecting plainspoken wisdom. And many a Sunday afternoon he took respite from the world of high finance by selling peanuts at Grand Prairie's Yello Belly Drag Strip.

When word of his passing hit the media, a few people might have gotten out their party clothes. Not because they were glad he was gone, but rather because O. L. had invited them one-and-all to a Texas-size bash. In 1968, Nelms had begun auctioning off most of his properties, telling reporters he intended to put the cash into a trust fund that would pay for a series of "dead man's parties" after his death. Plans called for the deceased businessman to be present at each party, laid out in a twenty-five-thousand-dollar silver casket. Instructions further stipulated that any heir who tried to have the casket buried instead of moved to the next party would be promptly disinherited. Nelms figured that each party would cost about one hundred thousand dollars. Inviting the general public, the businessman announced, "There will be no limit on the number of drinks a person could have. The only thing that would stop the liquor flowing to anybody would be bad behavior." Asked why he wanted so much drinking at the parties, Nelms replied, "Drinking people will tell you the truth. Sober people will lie to you."

Though the parties never occurred, O. L. made a national television appearance on *The Joe Pyne Show*, a late '60s pioneer of confrontational broadcasting, to explain the party plan. The fund, he said, would be administered by a self-perpetuating board of directors, and the parties would be held at least annually, but preferably four per year. It would be O. L. Nelms' way of saying, "Thank you, Dallas," forever.

19

Jim "Silver Dollar" West

O. L. Nelms, who tried to exhibit a million silver dollars at the State Fair of Texas, was not the only eccentric millionaire performance folk-artist deeply possessed by the spell of the elemental disc. To Jim "Silver Dollar" West, the eight-bit coin was not mere lucre, it was a magic ticket, a powerful symbol of the land that bore his name. And he greatly desired that others would savor its romantic allure, as well.

Custom pockets sewn into Silver Dollar's duds could hold as many as eighty of the chunky bucks. He used them as tips and as gifts of greeting wherever he went. When the spell was strongest, Jim would grab a handful and fling 'em to folks.

To the chagrin of Houston's less imaginative Big and Rich, Silver Dollar Jim liked to run around Texas "looking like a deputy sheriff out of an old western movie," as James Aswell described him in a 1953 *Collier's* profile. An Associated Press reporter marveled at Jim's monogrammed cowboy boots, gold-handled side arms in jeweled holsters, ornate gold belt buckles, and platinum collar points. Aswell rated Jim's headgear as "the 15 gallon Texas economy size." A treasured official Texas Ranger badge, rarely given to private citizens, adorned Jim's chest. As the badge was too small for silver dollars, Jim customized it with diamonds instead.

Guests at Silver Dollar Jim's Figure 2 Ranch, near Eagle Pass, could

"Silver Dollar" Jim, ready for action. Courtesy of *Collier's*.

belly up to the bar and play a slot machine rigged to pay off every time, probably in silver dollars. At his Madison County ranch in East Texas, Silver Dollar Jim, according to stories gathered by Frank X. Tolbert, often kept neighbors awake by blasting his country-western records all night long from a tower fitted with powerful loudspeakers. A portable sound system on a trailer allowed Jim to take his disc-jockey act on the road, rolling through Madisonville and North Zulch at four in the morning, serenading townsfolk with Hank Williams and Hank Thompson. For towns deprived of the comforting sound of trains passing in the night, Silver Dollar played records of railroad sound effects.

Next to silver dollars and country music, Jim loved law enforcement. He may have looked like an Old West sheriff, but he was definitely 1950s high-tech. Wherever he was at any given moment—in his bedroom, office, or the garages sheltering his dozens of customized automobiles—special radio and telephone units kept him informed of the latest developments in Houston's crime scene. Detectives rode the all-night beat with Jim, monitoring the streets in plush Cadillacs equipped with .28-gauge sawed-off shotguns, .30-.30 rifles, tommy guns, and state-of-the-art communications hardware. Houston legend has it that, during a shoot-out with a burglary suspect, the volunteer crime-fighter accidentally shot one detective in the foot.

With his reputation for passing the silver, Jim found himself constantly besieged with pleas for aid. One request he rewarded was from an eight-year-old Irish boy. The lad wrote a letter asking for a cowboy outfit and addressed it to "Any Millionaire, Houston." The post office delivered it to Silver Dollar. Believing that no one should go through life sans dude-ranch duds, Jim shipped the boy a complete western ensemble. A photo of the little buckaroo dressed for ridin' the range occupied an honored spot among the millionaire's mementos.

My old friend Sam Griswold also received the Silver Dollar treatment as a youngster as his parents were good friends with West's nurse and her husband. "I always thought he was kind of an honorary Texas Ranger," said Sam. "Department of Public Safety troopers brought him to our house in Dallas four times, always late at night, and we kids would be roused from our sleep to receive his greetings, a case of Snickers, and four or five nineteenth-century silver dollars. We were impressed beyond words and frozen in place."

A big believer in keeping an ace in the hole, Jim kept a whole casino-full up his sleeve. After his death from diabetes in 1957, executors of his River Oaks estate found 290,000 silver dollars secreted in his cellar vaults.

20

Bozo Texino

As Bozo Texino might say, one person's graffiti is another person's masterpiece. In the 1920s and '30s (and likely into the '40s), Bozo, whose real name was J. H. McKinley, created over 250,000 works of art that were viewed all over North America. A San Antonio locomotive fireman for the Missouri-Pacific Railroad, Texino created his distinctive doodles on the sides of boxcars in yellow waterproof crayon.

Bozo Texino, the boxcar artist at work. Courtesy of the *San Antonio Light* Collection, Institute of Texan Cultures.

The image, a figure smoking a pipe and wearing a ten-gallon hat with a star on it, appeared above the artist's signature.

The boxcar Picasso also wrote a humor column, "Bozo Texino Sez," in the railroad line's magazine. Of the difficulties of writing Bozo noted, "Believe me, a 40,000-pound freight locomotive is easier to operate than my seven-pound typewriter."

Texino told a reporter for the *San Antonio Light* in 1939 that a nephew nicknamed him Bo when they had worked together in Laredo. "I just took the 'Bo' and added a 'zo,' so it would go with Laredo. I used to sign it 'Bozo Laredo,' until I came to San Antonio, then kinda shortened Texas and Mexico to get 'Texino.'"

A second Bozo Texino carried on the tradition in the 1970s and '80s, but the drawings of the latter-day Bozo lack the star on the hat and feature a different type of pipe.

21

Ray's Ornamental Gardens

The creative mind, we are told, works in mysterious ways. None more mysterious, perhaps, has blossomed in the Texas sun than that of Stephenville philosopher-folk-artist George Ellis Ray (1881–1957). Ray's Ornamental Gardens, the folk-art environment George created fifty miles southwest of Fort Worth, was "a mecca for lovers of the unusual and the bizarre," according to a 1961 report in Stephenville's Tarleton State College newspaper.

As gospel music wafted from loudspeakers, garden visitors strolled through a wonderland of dozens of sculptural creations, formed of concrete and decorated with colored glass, tile, shell, rock, and petrified wood. Some of the pieces resembled ships' wheels, musical lyres, hearts, and stars, but others, as the Tarleton chronicler observed, "were of designs never before thought of." In toto, the works stood as abstract totems, somehow emblematic of the homemade proverbs that adorned signs placed throughout the outdoor gallery.

Stephenville artist George Ray stands among his installation of "designs never before thought of."

"Prejudice parks in an empty heart," preached one sign. "No man is above what he says about others," testified another. Some signs commented wryly on theology: "Everybody seems to believe in God after they work Him over to suit themselves." Another poetically contemplated the infinite, unreachable horizon of the human mind: "The further out on the sea of thought we go, the more we see that we don't know." For ten cents, visitors could buy a thirty-three-page souvenir booklet of the wise sayings titled *Rayisms*. Postcard views on sale at the site carried images of Ray's art across the country.

After Ruth Ray, George's widow, died in 1967, the gardens deteriorated more rapidly. At some point, Tarleton rodeo boys honed their roping skills on the ruins of the unusual creation. Today, only scattered fragments remain. According to local folklore, George left buried treasure in his garden galleries on the high bank of the Bosque River. But self-taught archeologist Alvis Delk, the current owner of the property, says the loot is nowhere to be found.

22

O. T. Nodrog, the Outer Dimensional Forces, and the Time Ark Service Modules

Strange objects and forces, it has oft been told, traveled through and descended from the vast Texas sky long before humankind first walked upon the land. By the cusp of the twentieth century, the unidentified atmospheric entities had evolved, along with an imaginative civilization, to the form of futuristic aircraft. In 1897, there were at least 104 reported sightings of a mysterious, ether-cruising vessel from Orange to El Paso, Paris to Eagle Pass. Most of the accounts by judges, lawmen, merchants, and other solid citizens described the 1897 UFO as cigar-shaped—some even specified a Mexican cigar. Echoing others, a Trinity County farmer reported "brilliant lights streaming from a ponderous vessel of strange proportions." Many non-witnesses probably agreed with one Dr. E. Sturat, an "expert on metaphysics," who attributed the craze to "hypnotism and bad whiskey."

In mid-April 1897, five days after the first sighting of the airship south of Dallas, a "Martian" died when his Marsmobile crashed into a windmill and water well in Aurora, north of Dallas. The man from Mars was buried in the Aurora cemetery the next day. At least that's the story that Auroran S. E. Hayden told the *Dallas Morning News*.

Apparently this news failed to stir up much excitement. Years later, Wise County historian Etta Pegues wrote in her book, *Aurora, Texas: The Town that Might Have Been*, that Hayden had concocted the story to draw tourists to the small town. It worked, too, but not until some seventy years later, when Dallas columnist Frank X. Tolbert unearthed the Martian mystery. Soon, British investigators from *Flying Saucer Review* trekked to Aurora, joining UFOlogists from far and near in pestering the locals and poking around the cemetery.

Researchers considered exhuming the Martian, but no one knew the exact grave site (nor would cemetery officials consent). And the well where the alleged crash had occurred had long been cemented over, its owner fearing that Martian radiation had aggravated his arthritis. Later analysis of metal fragments retrieved near the well indicated they had once been part of a 1920s stove, though Wallace O. Chariton reported in his 1991 book, *The Great Texas Airship Mystery*, that one metal tester "admitted privately that the crystalline structure of the metal was unlike anything he had ever seen."

In the modern, post-Roswell UFO era, there have been innumerable sightings across the state. A mysterious document that UFOlogists call Majic-12 or MJ-12 mentions one such. The document's top-secret text, which identifies it as having been prepared by the CIA for President-elect Eisenhower, describes the dozen-member Majestic-12 group formed to study the UFO phenomenon two months after the Roswell crash of 1947. Though it has never been conclusively proven that MJ-12 was an authentic CIA document, its text described the four dead occupants of the Roswell crash craft as "human-like in appearance," though "the biological and evolutionary processes responsible for their development have apparently been quite different from those observed or postulated in homo sapiens." Majestic-12 adopted the term "Extra-terrestrial Biological Entities, or EBEs." MJ-12 was similarly stumped by the craft's method of flight, finding a "complete absence of wings, propellers, jets or other conventional methods of propulsion and guidance, as well as a total lack of metallic wiring, vacuum tubes or other similar recognizable electronic components."

Then the document mentions a related event that has received much less attention than the Roswell crash: "On 06 December, 1950, a second object, probably of similar origin, impacted the earth at high speed in the El Indio-Guerrero area of the Texas-Mexican border [south of Eagle Pass and Piedras Negras] after following a long trajectory through the atmosphere. By the time a search team arrived, what remained of the object had been almost totally incinerated. Such material as could be recovered was transported to the A.E.C. facility at Sandia, New Mexico, for study."

In 1964, my own musician father later reported, he observed a flying saucer descending into the cornfield of his Dallas County farm, as he arrived home from a gig in the middle of the night. Around the same

O. T. Nodrog sells honey and avocado plants, while soliciting "Real Human Beings!" to join his "Armageddon Time Ark Base Operation," at the Weslaco Flea Market, circa 1982. Photo by and courtesy of Douglas Curran.

time, down on the Rio Grande, Orville T. Gordon, aka O. T. Nodrog, was keeping his eyes peeled for the appearance of Time Ark Service Modules. Mixing his own creative sci-fi lingo with biblical prophecy, Nodrog and his associates at the Armageddon Time Ark Base of Weslaco awaited an apocalyptic S-Day, when Yahweh would activate the sixth seal of the book of Revelation and all hades would break loose.

Writer/photographer Douglas Curran interpreted the group's vision in his 1985 book, *In Advance of the Landing.* "Early on the morning of S-Day," explained Curran, "the cosmic fleet will effect a six-degree shift in the Earth's polar alignment. The Manasseh Complex [North America], shuddering and convulsing, will move eastward as earthquakes crack open the land and the seas inundate the continent. To the west of present-day Weslaco will arise a new mountain draining off the flooded valley of the lower Rio Grande. This valley will be the new Eden, the City Foursquare envisioned in Revelations 21:16." The one percent of the world's population that had undergone the group's survival training would be rescued from the cataclysm by the Time Ark Service Modules, which had already begun to, as Nodrog put it, "functionate interdimensional power exchange."

Orville T. Gordon came to the Rio Grande Valley from Wisconsin in the 1930s and opened a lumberyard in Weslaco, according to data gathered by Douglas Curran. After conflicts with local and federal tax authorities in the early 1960s, Gordon closed the business and began expanding his philosophical horizons. As Orville T. Gordon transformed himself into O. T. Nodrog, the lumberyard morphed into the Armageddon Time Ark Base Operation. In 1963, according to Nodrog literature, Yahshua Hamashiia, said to be the son of the Creator, Yahweh, ordained Nodrog as Earth Coordinator, or channeler, of the Outer Dimensional Forces. When hurricanes Beulah and Fern roared up the Rio Grande in 1967, Nodrog interpreted their fury as the whirlwind of Christ from Isaiah 66:15. "Humatons," Nodrog argued, had "perverfractioneered" the teachings of the Bible.

When Douglas Curran met Nodrog in 1982, the Santa-whiskered visionary was selling avocado plants, wheat berries, and honey at the Weslaco flea market. He also passed out fliers soliciting "Real Human Beings! Positive Pioneers Who are Capable of Facing the Reality of The Time Frontier and Redeveloping and Repopulating the Manasseh Complex." Though Nodrog stated that "A.T.A. Base Operations is not interested in UFOs, but rather, [is] involved in ISOs (Identified Sailing Objects)," a recruiting poster displayed at the flea market offered a "PASSPORT TO SURVIVAL" above a drawing of a flying saucer. The A.T.A.B.O. Cosmic Corps of Engineers stationery also featured drawings of conventional flying saucers, along with a map of the Rio Grande running through a mystic star that included the paths of Beulah and Fern.

Despite the overwrought neologisms and hyperbolic prophecy, Nodrog made some good points about the excesses and abuses of Big Brother and organized religion. The group withdrew from the public eye in the 1990s, but in 1999, news reports quoted a 90-year-old Nodrog warning that North America was headed for trouble. On New Year's Eve, as the clock ticked toward 2000, a McAllen newspaper, the *Monitor*, dispatched a reporter to stake out the Armageddon Time Ark Base Operation headquarters, but the Outer Dimensional Forces and Time Ark Service Modules were nowhere to be seen.

PART TWO

OTHER TEXAS CHARACTERS

23

A Pair of Snake Kings and One Snake Queen

Fairgoers at the 1893 World's Columbian Exposition in Chicago stood breathless and bug-eyed at the rattlesnake-killing booth of Clark Stanley, Texas cowboy turned medicine man. Attired in picturesque western garb, Stanley held crowds spellbound as he methodically slaughtered hundreds of the notorious reptiles and processed the juices into his quick-selling, sure-cure Snake Oil Liniment.

At least, that's how he tells it in his curious pamphlet, *The Life and Adventures of the American Cowboy: True Life in the Far West by Clark Stanley, Better Known as the Rattlesnake King.*

First published in 1897, various editions of the booklet include the King's life story, some peculiar information on the cowboy life, lyrics for cowboy songs, and advertisements for Stanley's White Cactus Soap, Western Herbs, and the old stand-by, Clark Stanley's Snake Oil Liniment, said to be "good for man and beast."

Claiming to be a native of Abilene, Texas, Stanley wrote that he made his first trip up the cattle trail at age fourteen and that he followed the cowboy life for eleven years. In the spring of 1879, Stanley chronicled, he traveled to the Arizona settlement of Wolpi (he probably meant Walpi) to witness the snake dance of the Moki Pueblo. According to Frank Waters' *Book of the Hopi*, Moki is the name of the Hopi Deer Clan. (Stanley's biggest problem here is that Abilene, Texas, was not founded until about 1880.)

In the Moki Pueblo, the Rattlesnake King explained, "I became acquainted with the medicine man of the Moki tribe, and as he liked the looks of my Colt revolver . . . I gave him an exhibition of my fancy shooting, which pleased him very much." After witnessing the dramatic snake dance, the young cowboy was so impressed that he stayed with the Indians two and a half years.

He learned their language and dances, he writes, and the secret of making their medicines. The medicine that interested him most was their Snake Oil Medicine, as Stanley reported they called it, which the Moki used for rheumatism, colds, and all other aches and pains.

"As I was thought of a great deal by the medicine man, he gave me the secret of making the Snake Oil Medicine," Stanley related. "Snake Oil is not a new discovery. It has been in use by the Mokis and other Indian tribes for many generations, and I have made improvements on the original formula," Stanley wrote. The reputed cowboy doesn't say whether he swapped his own medicinal remedy with the Indians—an old Texas folk remedy of tying a dead rattlesnake around a sufferer's head.

Taking leave of the Mokis, Stanley returned to Abilene—the story goes—and unleashed the wonders of Snake Oil on a rheumatism epidemic. Folks perked up so much that he began manufacturing Clark Stanley's Snake Oil Liniment in bulk and hit the road to hawk the magnificent elixir. At the Chicago World's Fair, East Coast druggists lured him to Providence, Rhode Island, where he established a factory to produce Snake Oil Liniment and his other products. Some snakes were raised in Rhode Island, but most—the Rattlesnake King advertised—were shipped to the factory from his snake farm back in Texas.

Though it is possible, if not likely, that Stanley never saw the Moki snake dance, visions of exotic ceremonies in the faraway land of Arizona must have enchanted metropolitan dwellers as they read of thrilling western adventures in the Rattlesnake King's booklet while soothing their neuralgia and lumbago with Snake Oil Liniment. The Rhode Island snake oil magnate noted that many of his fellow Easterners felt that the West was "not a good place for peaceable and law-abiding people." But he insisted that a reading of his book would quickly dispel "the false illusions of a large percentage of Eastern people in regard to the habits and customs of the so-called wild and wooly Westerners."

Stanley's text sought to explain, for an Eastern audience, the cowboy appearance and attire, why they wore the big hats, spurs, bandanas, and high-heeled boots, and why they carried guns. Perhaps most confusing was the serpent king's description of the cowboy coiffure. "As to long hair there are good reasons why the cowboys wear it," Stanley expounded.

> Their business is out of doors, rain or shine, and in many changes of climate, and they have found from experience that the greatest protection to the eyes and ears is long hair. Old miners and hunters know this well. Scouts, hunters, trailers and guides let their hair grow as a rule. Those who have been prejudiced against it have suffered the conse-

Claiming to be a native of Abilene and to have learned the secrets of snake oil from Moki Indians, Clark Stanley, aka the Rattlesnake King, dressed western to advertise his Rhode Island–produced patent medicine. Courtesy of the Center for American History, the University of Texas at Austin, CN06250.

quences of pains in the head, sore eyes, and a loud ringing noise in the ears. A result of exposure without the protection of long hair is loss of hearing in one ear, caused by one or the other of the ears being exposed more when the cowboy is lying on the ground. Healthy hearing and eyesight are of the greatest importance to the cowboy, scout or hunter. There are some white men whose interests call them to live among the Indians, and it is a fact that by letting their hair grow long they gain favor with the people they live among.

For those inspired by his tales "My Last Trip Up The Trail" and "The Texas Kid," author Stanley included how-to information on obtaining land in Texas and getting started in the cattle baron business. The booklet's handy fill-in-the-blanks homesteading affidavits whetted the Go West urge even more.

Other sections covered "Character in the Handshake," and a trip Stanley reportedly made to Washington, D.C., in 1905 to ride in Teddy Roosevelt's inaugural parade with other "old-time" cowboys. The President greeted the saddle-sitting punchers warmly. "This is the proudest day of my life," the Rattlesnake King told the Executive Rough Rider. At the greeting's conclusion the group of cowboys gathered by a White House portico and serenaded Roosevelt with "three shrill cowboy yells."

Some editions of the Rattlesnake King's booklet contained lyrics of cowboy songs and an essay on songs and dances of the range country. But as Guy Logsdon points out in his 1990 book, *The Whorehouse Bells Were Ringing*, Stanley's text appears to be plagiarized word for word from an article by Grace Ward in *Pearson's Magazine*. "It was probable," noted Logsdon, "that Stanley had never been a cowboy" and that his text on life in the West was plagiarized as well.

Gerald Carson, the late historian of American medical theatrics, wrote in *One for a Man, Two for a Horse*, that Stanley's Snake Oil Liniment was misnamed. Carson stated that government chemists had determined that the nostrum contained kerosene, camphor, and "turps." But no snake sauce.

Decades after Stanley's death, researchers undertook serious investigations to learn whether a form of snake oil might prove more efficacious than Stanley himself could ever have dreamed. Biotech labs in the 1980s studied rattlesnake venom in an effort to clone proteins that might someday retard the growth of human tumors.

Another future member of reptile royalty appeared at the 1893 Chicago World's Fair when fifteen-year-old Willie Lieberman, a Brooklyn native, came looking for work. Taking a job as the "wild man" in a cage of live snakes for a midway show, the boy began his life's work. After deciding that reptiles and other wild animals were his calling, Lieberman worked for or met almost every snake exhibitor in the country during the next few years. Called "geek shows" at the time, the serpentine entertainments always had a pressing need for more fresh snakes. Sizing up the opportunity, young Lieberman envisioned a vast snake farm shipping live specimens to showmen all over the country.

Texas seemed a likely place for snakes to flourish, so Lieberman headed for the silvery Rio Grande. He didn't stop until he hit Brownsville at the state's southernmost tip. In 1907, the tropical borderlands outpost became the home of Snakeville, a name that would soon become known from coast to coast and beyond.

William Abraham Lieberman legally transformed to W. A. Snake King and began shipping reptiles to shows and carnivals as fast as the young rails could carry them north from Brownsville. The "Wild Horse Desert," as the region around Brownsville was called, didn't have rail service until about 1904.

In the early days at Snakeville, King had to capture most of the snakes himself, though he did get some from local suppliers. One of these hunters soon became Mrs. Snake King. "Women are better snake hunters than men," Mr. Snake King told a reporter in 1910. "I'd rather wear dresses and skirts than trousers in snake hunting, for the snake springs and hangs onto the skirts, and thus hanging he is practically helpless. She reaches down and gets him without danger, if she is quick."

Soon a network of hunters on both sides of the border kept the wholesaler supplied with almost enough to meet the growing demand. Orders arrived from everywhere. One reptile request found its way to Brownsville with no more addressee indication than a drawing of a snake over the scrawled letters "TEXAS" and "USA."

The Snake King became a master promoter and publicist, and the press found he made for spiffy copy wherever he went. When he ran

W. A. Snake King shipped rattlers and other wild animals worldwide from his Brownsville snake farm. Photo by Robert Runyon, courtesy of the Center for American History, the University of Texas at Austin, Robert Runyan Photograph Collection, RUN 08076.

into Will Rogers once at an Oklahoma fair, the Cherokee Cowboy mentioned in passing the sensational season then being enjoyed by Babe Ruth. Exhibiting the strict focus the serpent dealer held on his business, King earnestly replied, "Who's he? Does he sell snakes?"

For a 1914 promotion stunt, the Snake King rode a donkey from Snakeville to the state capitol in Austin. Wearing a huge sombrero, the five-foot-two-inch Snake King rode the burro right up the steps of the granite statehouse. As son W. A. King Jr. recalled fifty years later in his book *Rattling Yours, Snake King*, "That year Brownsville was preparing to put on its Sixth Annual Mid-Winter Fair. To add color to the event, Dad proposed a Rattlesnake Catching Contest." The invitation Snake King delivered to the governor "was branded on a tanned bobcat skin, then gift-wrapped in a large Texas rattlesnake skin topped by a matching bow tie. Everybody in town turned out to give Dad a royal send-off . . . That was one day, old timers recall, when tequila and mescal flowed freely. A brass band blasted away noisily, its not-so-good music sharply punctuated by 45s fired in the air."

Snake King's colorful stationery depicted Mr. and Mrs. Snake King—"This is me. This is her."—framed by intertwined rattlers and prickly pear cactus. Checks sent from the Snake King office were printed with a snake running the length of the payee blank so that the recipient's name was written on the serpent's body.

The resourceful Snake King found a market for dead rattlesnakes as well as live ones. Venom went for thirty-two dollars an ounce for use in making antidotes. Skins brought seventy-five cents a foot and rattles ten cents an inch. Skulls sold for four dollars and fifty cents, and gall bladders bottled in wine fetched two dollars.

In time, the Snake King expanded his inventory to include javelinas, iguanas, lions, apes, parrots, elephants, and other wild creatures. A terrible flood hit the Rio Grande in September 1933, washing iguanas, imported from Mexico, all over the Brownsville area. Decades later, descendants of these big lizards flourished in the region. Stuffed horned toads became a big seller in 1928 when a horned toad named Old Rip made headlines after being "discovered alive" in a cornerstone of the Eastland County courthouse, where he'd been sealed back in 1897.

The exotic bird business conducted by Snake King had an unexpected impact. He discovered that many of the birds, imported from far south of the border, were being sold off along the way by rail employees. To stop this practice, large tags were affixed to the crates of parrots, stating that the birds were contaminated and should not be handled until vaccinated.

When U.S. officials got wind of the situation, the parrot fever craze was born. "Dad challenged the U.S. Public Health Bureau, through the nation's press, to stop the gobbledygook and prove that such a fever actually existed," wrote W. A. King Jr. But the only result was strict regulation of parrot importation with periods of quarantine and federal inspection. The episode continues to affect border affairs as smuggling of the valuable birds is today a profitable, illegal enterprise.

Other wild adventures chronicled in the entertaining *Rattling Yours*

W. D. Smithers wrote that his friend, Leona Learn, who sold reptiles in San Antonio, had survived more than a thousand rattlesnake bites. She is shown here, wrote Smithers, in her "native Cherokee Indian dress." Photo by W. D. Smithers, courtesy of the Harry Ransom Humanities Research Center, University of Texas at Austin.

(the closing phrase of Snake King's letters) include circus tours of Mexico, a bizarre Hollywood film company that shot the classic "Death Along the Delta" near Snakeville, and the exhibition of "Big Boy, The Giant Gorilla" at the 1928 Democratic National Convention in Houston.

Author W. A. King Jr. proves himself just as imaginative as his colorful father, though certainly more modest. The traditional author's photo in King's book shows only the back of his head, described by King as "my best view."

Another rattler emporium flourished in San Antonio. The city's 1918 directory listed a W. O. Learn and Co., managed by Martha Learn, at 504 Dolorosa, which offered "Texas and Mexican reptiles, parrots, and wild animals." By 1926, the W. Odell Learn Co. had relocated to 414 S. Flores.

The Learns' daughter, Leona, became so famed in the snake world that Harry Houdini mentioned her in his 1920 book, *Miracle Mongers and Their Methods: A Complete Exposé.* "This lady deals in live rattlesnakes and their by-products," wrote Houdini, "rattlesnake skin, which is used for fancy bags and purses; rattlesnake oil, which is highly esteemed in some quarters as a specific for rheumatism; and the venom, which has a pharmaceutical value." Leona Learn told the escape artist that she had imparted her secrets to the well-known "rattlesnake poison defier" and stage-and-sideshow performer named Thardo. Thardo wowed the crowds by allowing rattlers to plunge their fangs into her skin and inject the deadly venom with no ill effects.

Photographer W. D. Smithers knew Leona Learn in the mid-1920s, estimating her to be about fifty years old and the "most famous" snake dealer in the state and perhaps beyond. "Leona, when a small girl, was trained as a snake charmer by her mother, who was with a circus," wrote Smithers. "She estimated that she had been bitten more than a thousand times. She willingly offered to let a rattlesnake strike her on her cheek, then, to prove that the snake did have a big supply of venom, she milked the snake for the rest of its supply, enough to have killed a couple of persons."

24

Giants

It's unclear when the folklore about the "Long Tall Texan" first took root, but in a late-nineteenth-early-twentieth century sideshow tradition, a long line of tall drinks of water from the big state trekked from Hobokenville, New York, to East Saginaw, Michigan, and beyond, where the public paid good money to gawk at their gigantism.

The four Shields brothers of White Rock, Texas, had already soared to heights ranging from seven-feet-eight-inches to just shy of eight feet when they joined a Barnum & Bailey sideshow around 1880. Shade, Guss, Frank, and Jack Shields each made about six dollars a day as "The Texas Giants." The brothers sold souvenir photos of their skyscraper frames, and Guss wrote a little book about attaining such high altitude.

Three of the brothers returned to Texas after ten years, but Shade trouped on into the 1890s. At one point he and wife Annie were billed as "The Texas Giant and Giantess." Retired from the torchlights, Shade and Guss ran a saloon in Greenville. But in his last years, recalling the magic of the big top, Shade spent most of his time on Missouri riverboats with his good friend and fellow circus veteran, thirty-six-inch-tall Major Ray, who had previously formed one half of what was billed as the smallest married couple in the world.

Terrell native Tex Baker amazed circus-goers around 1910 with stories of eleven inches of growth in seven months; Tex wound up at about eight-feet-two-inches tall. Texas Slim Page, a mere 7'6", nonetheless was ballyhooed as "the world's tallest cowboy." J. G. Tarver of Dallas, variously reported at 8'6" and 8'2", appeared with Ringling Bros. and other circuses as "Big Jim Tarver, the Texas Giant" from 1907 to 1933.

At 8'6", Jacob Erlich, better known as Jack Earle, appeared in forty-eight movies before he took to the circus trail. Ironically, Jacob had been so small at birth that doctors feared he wouldn't survive. In 1926, while at home in El Paso attending college, friends took him to the circus to see Big Jim Tarver. A sideshow recruiter followed Jack home, and that fall, he debuted in Madison Square Garden. Earle toured with various incarnations of "The Greatest Show on Earth" for fourteen years. In his

TEXAS GIANTS.
THE SHIELDS BROTHERS.

SHADE.	GUSS.	FRANK.	JACK.
Height, 7 ft. 8 in.	7 ft. 10 in.	7 ft. 11¾ in.	7 ft. 11¾ in.
Age, 18	24	24	

Willes Photo.   Balto.

The Shields brothers traveled the land as some of the most famous tall Texans.

Jay Little, "Texas Giant Boy," seems a little shy for the showbiz life.

post-circus life, the melancholy giant became a traveling wine salesman and dabbled in photography, writing poetry, and oil painting.

Like his fellow circus performers of uncommon size, Jack Earle faced a challenge in finding the right "fit" in life—whether it was clothing or his coffin. Though he adopted a philosophical view of his station in life, the thoughtless behavior of some "normal" folks still wounded his sensitive nature. He probably found solace in the wisdom of his friend Harry Doll, a circus performer known for his diminutiveness. "Don't worry, Jack," counseled Harry, "there are more freaks out there in the crowd than there are up here."

25

Big Sam

Untold numbers of skyscraping gents toured the country as "Texas Giants," but at least one Lone Star son won fame for his horizontal dimensions. Vertically, Sam Harris (1873–1924) of Farmersville soared to a mere 6'2". But in his prime, carnival barkers described the 731-pound "Texas Kid" as the "World's Heaviest Man."

Farmersville historian Charlie Rike wrote that Sam began to pack on the pounds after suffering from typhoid fever as a young man. Fully-grown, Harris served for a time as the town marshal. His intimidating size made it unnecessary to carry a weapon, and he could simply pick up a lawbreaker and tote him off to jail. Resisting arrest, folks say, was unheard of in the days when Marshal Sam wore the star.

Locals marveled at the strength of "Big Sam" for decades after his death, and even today Farmersville mayor Robbin Lamkin says the big man is "a legend in this area." Old-timers recall stories about Sam entering a burning building to push a safe weighing a ton out of the conflagration. Sam himself allowed that he could "lift anything that is loose at both ends."

Serving as mascot for the Farmersville Woodmen of the World, Sam even caught the attention of world-weary New Yorkers when he sauntered through the Big Apple in his custom W.O.W. uniform, carrying a

SAM HARRIS
TEX-KID
FARMERSVILLE, TEXAS
HEAVIEST MAN LIVING, WEIGHT 691 LBS.

Big Sam Harris of Farmersville gained renown for his horizontal dimensions.

giant axe that looked borrowed from Paul Bunyan. *Ripley's Believe It or Not!* increased his renown when it weighed in on his Texas-size frame around 1920.

Like extra-tall Texans, extra-wide Sam had to have his clothing and furniture specially made. He rode around Farmersville in a one-of-a-kind buggy pulled by a team of white mules or in a custom truck that featured a canopy over a platform with a settee in the center. Years before his death from pneumonia at age fifty-one, Sam ordered a coffin built large enough to sleep four men of average size. Charlie Rike recorded that some ten thousand people attended Sam's funeral. Too large for a hearse, Sam took his final ride in a truck.

Interviewed in 1964, Sam's son John said people still stopped in Farmersville from all over the country to inquire about his larger-than-life pop. John recalled him as "just a good father . . . He used to take us swimming a lot. He would float on his back while us kids climbed up on him and dived off."

Others also remembered the "jovial giant" fondly. "You might say," added local feed store owner Coleman Jennings, "that most of him was heart."

26

Stout Jackson

Billed in his prime as "Stout Jackson: World's Greatest Strong Man, Greatest One Man Show On Earth," Thomas Jefferson Jackson (1890–1976) began pumping iron as a smaller-than-average youth, inspired by other kids' teasing and by the clean-living principles handed down by his Baptist-preacher father.

The Jack County ranch where Jackson was raised provided ample opportunity for strength-building workouts, and he debuted professionally at age seventeen in nearby Joplin. The "Stoutest Man Living" pulled cars with his teeth, drove nails with his fist, and played tug-of-war with horses. He first toured by mule-drawn wagon through Texas and Oklahoma, but was soon traveling by train, boat, and Model T

Stout Jackson in action. Courtesy the Todd-McLean Physical Culture Collection.

throughout the country, into Canada, and to South America. At times, he performed with circuses.

From 1919 to 1935, Stout and his family (he had a wife and son by then) lived in Lubbock, where he may have performed a feat unequaled in the annals of pump-you-up-itude: in 1924, Stout back-lifted twelve cotton bales, which weighed in at the all-time record of 6,472 pounds—at least, that's how *Ripley's Believe It Or Not!* reported the lift in 1949. Some historians dispute the claim. "Many strongmen exaggerated," noted Kimberly Ayn Beckwith in a 1994 issue of *Iron Game History*, "to add flair to their show and attract crowds."

In a scenario that was probably repeated around the state, two brothers in Lohn tried to perform Stout's rope-breaking-with-bare-hands trick and wound up with hernias.

In 1935, Stout, by then semi-retired from the "iron game," moved with his wife, Beatrice, to Robstown. Noticing a lack of Spanish-language entertainment venues, Stout opened a string of *teatros carpas*, or tent theaters, in Robstown, Alice, Kingsville, and Falfurrias. He showed films imported from Mexico and arranged for personal appearances by Mexican marquee idols. He also built a few permanent theater structures.

The Jackson family served South Texas' Hispanic majority in many other ways, including Beatrice's work as a midwife. It's said that many a Tejana around Robstown today is named Beatrice.

27

Milt Hinkle

Aerial Bulldogger

Taught the rodeo art of bulldogging—in which a contestant leaps onto a running steer from his horse and wrestles it to the ground— by its inventor, Bill Pickett, cowboy Milt Hinkle added his own innovations. But it wasn't until a 1931 rodeo in Nuevo Laredo that Milt discovered that aerial bulldogging was a whole 'nother matter.

Known as "Mr. Rodeo" and "The South American Kid," Milt Hinkle (1881–1972) began life on the XIT Ranch, and spent some of his early years in Grapevine where he became a ranch hand at age nine. According to Hinkle legend, young Milt took first place in bronc riding six years later at his first rodeo and remained hooked on cowboy athletics for the rest of his long life. His western showbiz career reportedly included seven years with Buffalo Bill's outfit.

Announcing Hinkle's appearance at the rodeo held in Nuevo Laredo during the 1931 Washington's Birthday Celebration, the *Laredo Times* credited Milt with the world's record (sixty-eight miles per hour) for bulldogging from a speeding automobile.

A cowboy who was scheduled to bulldog from an airplane flying out of Nuevo Laredo came down, understandably, with a sudden illness. Milt reluctantly agreed to stand in for the "aerial rodeo" star, though he

Milt Hinkle, long after that fateful day in Nuevo Laredo. Courtesy of the Center for American History, the University of Texas at Austin, CN08316.

suggested to the pilot that they'd best head northward from the Rio Grande.

According to the *Laredo Times*, the bull turned and charged the plane as it swooped in low with Mr. Rodeo dangling from the landing gear. *El toro* wrecked the Ryan aircraft, then staggered off the field. Though the *Times* stated that Milt was not seriously hurt, he sustained leg injuries that effectively crippled him.

Showing true western grit, after the accident Milt segued into the role of rodeo producer and colorful character, traveling across the country from his home in Kissimmee, Florida, where he helped found the Silver Spurs Rodeo.

In the last decade of his life, Milt chronicled the wild old days in reminiscences told on television and published in magazines like *True West*, *Old West*, and *Frontier Times*. Sometimes going by the name Uncle Milt, he spun yarns of his association with Bat Masterson, Annie Oakley, Butch Cassidy, Will Rogers, O. Henry, Teddy Roosevelt, and dozens of other celebrities. And at rodeos everywhere, the cowboy-hatted octogenarian never failed to enthrall youngsters when he stuck out a friendly hand and declared, "Shake the hand that shook the hand of Wyatt Earp."

28

Booger Red

"Ugliest Man Dead or Alive"

There ain't no horse that can't be rode, and there ain't no rider that can't be throwed.

If you believe the stories about Samuel Thomas "Booger Red" Privett (1864–1924), the second part of that old saying is all hat. Raised on a ranch near Dublin in Erath County, by age twelve Privett had gained a reputation clear into Palo Pinto County as "The Redheaded Kid Bronc Rider."

A gunpowder accident in 1877 marred the thirteen-year-old's face and inspired his nickname. A neighbor boy climbed up into the wagon as the family carried Samuel Thomas to the doctor. "Gee," said the boy, "Red sure is a booger." As Red convalesced, his brothers repeated the line; it seemed to give him comfort, and the name stuck.

Orphaned at fifteen, Booger Red became a professional broncobuster who drifted from ranches to rodeos to Wild West shows. He

Booger Red, seen here with his wife Mollie, was rarely photographed. Courtesy of Jim Lanning.

owned a small ranch near Sabinal for a time, but the lure of the road proved too strong. Booger tried to settle down again in 1895, when he married expert horsewoman Mollie Webb in Bronte, bought a wagon yard and horse-trading post in San Angelo, and fathered six children. But eventually, the whole family went on the road to perform in Booger Red's Wild West Show.

As Mollie explained to a WPA interviewer in the late 1930s, Booger Red was the first bronco-buster to ride with his thumbs in his suspenders, looking back over his shoulder to talk to the crowd. Another eyewitness recalled that he "rode the outlaws with his hands in the air, shouting at the joy of being alive." ("Outlaw" was a common term for a hard-to-ride horse.) Rodeo fan Gertie Fry said that when Booger rode a bronc, he "stuck like a flea on a flop-eared hound."

Yet another rodeo fan wrote that Booger's eyes "looked like two small caliber bullet holes in a sun-burned pumpkin." But cowboy Privett sought to put others at ease by joking about his condition. He always ended his pre-show pitch with, "Come and see him ride, the ugliest man dead or alive, Booger Red."

Booger rode the arenas into his fifties, finally retiring around the time of World War I to a ranch in Miami, Oklahoma. A short time before his death in 1924, he attended the Fort Worth Fat Stock Show. After one particularly rowdy outlaw bronc had thrown every rodeo cowboy who climbed aboard, a murmur in the crowd rose to a clamor, calling for Booger Red. So the "ridinest, ropinest cowpuncher in the West" climbed down from the stands to show 'em how it was done, one more time. For decades, folks who claimed to have been there circulated stories of "Booger Red's Last Ride."

Samuel Thomas Privett was inducted into the National Rodeo Hall of Fame in Oklahoma City in 1973. Twenty years earlier, an article in *The Cattleman* had summed up his final tally. "Booger Red," wrote Ervin Hickman, "is to the cowboy industry what Paul Bunyan is to the lumber industry and Popeye is to the spinach growers."

True to his legend, Booger Red showed his good-natured humor even in his dying words. Advising his children to be honest, "for it pays in the long run," he urged a practical approach to the gift of life: "Have all the fun you can while you live, for when you are dead you are a long-time dead."

Buck Gunter found his locks to be an asset with Buffalo Bill's Wild West Show. Courtesy of Lorene Milner.

Buck Gunter

Raisin' Hair and Ridin' Broncs

Texas males who grew their hair long in the 1960s often found life difficult in terms of employment and harassment. But at least one older Texan, Doc Weatherford Gunter, may have enjoyed the revival of extended cranial fuzz for menfolk. As a young man, long hair provided Buck the opportunity of a lifetime.

In 1903, eighteen-year-old Gunter left his native Jack County to seek adventure farther west. After landing a job as a bronco-buster on a Colorado ranch, he got a chance to try out for Buffalo Bill's Wild West extravaganza. Riding a particularly ornery outlaw that had "never been rode," the young cowboy impressed the show's manager, who hired him on the spot. Doc hadn't been into town to see a barber in at least six months, explaining that he grew his locks for protection against the wind and cold out on the range. Buffalo Bill told him to keep the tresses, nicknamed him Buck for his horseback bravado, and sometimes had him don a skirt when the female trick rider couldn't perform. Even in the Wild West, the show must go on.

Buck rode for Buffalo Bill for two years before breaking his leg coming out of the chute. He then returned home to Texas, where he worked on ranches in Jack and Palo Pinto counties. A lifelong lover of horses, Buck was still saddling up close to his dying day.

Samuel E. "Doc" Asbury

Texas Nativist

In his forty-five-year career as assistant state chemist, Samuel E. "Doc" Asbury (1872–1962) studied the science of matter, but his passion was the arts, especially the homegrown variety.

In 1914, Doc published his philosophy in a short-lived monthly magazine, *The Texas Nativist*, wherein he zestfully argued for support of all native Texas arts and industries. A Texas nativist, he decreed, needn't have been born in the state, but must dress in garments of Texas wool and cotton, enjoy Texas food, and long for Texas music, art, and architecture. In the dramatic realm, he called for musicals about the Alamo, La Bahía, and San Jacinto. "And from time to time," added Doc, "we shall attempt destructive criticism of evil tendencies in the dramas which come into Texas from the Eastern cities."

Shortly after World War I, Doc Asbury started his magnum opus, a Wagnerian-length opera on the Texas Revolution. In a 1929 speech at SMU, he testified, "Only by music—music in the folk-manner of the time of the Texas Revolution—may the heart of revolutionary Texas be revealed to the heart of our time, or its soul join the twentieth-century soul."

Though Doc never finished the opera, he labored on it for nearly half a century in a rose-covered cottage near the Texas A&M University campus. Visitors had to squeeze in sideways because of books piled everywhere and the four upright pianos in the front room. Framed prints and photographs covered all wall space, ceilings, and appliances. Doc also displayed designs for an octagonal performance space, explaining that the opera's action would take place on eight stages simultaneously.

Today, plans for the grand production reside in Doc Asbury's papers at the University of Texas and the Texas State Library, perhaps waiting for some twenty-first-century composer to bring the work to life.

Quinta Mazatlan

Adobe Outpost in the Rio Grande Valley

"They were both such good genuine people, but they were different," recalled one McAllen resident in 1984 of local mavericks
Jason Matthews (1887–1964) and his wife, Marcia Matthews
(1891–1963). "Jason was an odd character. I remember that well," added
another informant.

Memories of the pair were collected for the application for a Texas
Historical Commission marker for the Matthews' distinctive adobe
home, Quinta Mazatlan. Research into the "mystique" surrounding the
Matthews and Quinta Mazatlan led Rio Grande Valley historians
Robert E. Norton and Marjorie Lohner to conclude that "it is difficult
to sort out what is possibly fantasy and what is true fact, some of [the
enigma] being a characteristic of the Matthews themselves."

Truth and legend both began to circulate as soon as the couple
arrived in McAllen in the late 1930s. Jason presented an exotic image,
strolling to the post office each day in his Bermuda shorts with a walking stick, his goatee waving in the wind. Decades later, folks recalled stories that Jason had been an accomplished aviator, writer, photographer,
explorer, archaeologist, and composer, with connections to *National
Geographic* and the Smithsonian. Rumor had it that he had also seen
considerable action as a soldier of fortune in Africa and the Middle East.

Concern over global political instability, some said, led him to settle
in the Rio Grande Valley, which Matthews perceived as the crossroads
of the western hemisphere. Other locals opined that Jason built Quinta
Mazatlan on a hill so that he could more effectively spot planes for the
Germans in the early 1940s.

Whatever the rationale, many in McAllen sized Jason up as a few
bricks short of a load when he began constructing the ten-thousand-
square-foot adobe home and compound south of town. Mixing the
mud in an old cement mixer and a decrepit washing machine, the new-
comer used his own secret formula for the adobe, which Jason told folks
he found in the Bible. Some versions indicate that it was an adobe for-

mula used to build King Nebuchadnezzar's palace. It is generally believed that he mixed white lime with local clay for his twelve-inch-thick adobe bricks. Whatever the ingredients, McAllen wags cracked that the house would melt and wash away with the first heavy rain. Yet Quinta Mazatlan still stands today, stout as ever, welcoming visitors as part of the World Birding Center. Nature trails wind through the estate's eight acres of native flora and fauna. Guides point out that Jason painted the interior and exterior walls with aluminum sulphate paint to keep radar waves from penetrating his domain.

Guests during the Matthews era remembered "dress up" dinners with elegant silver. "Everyone stopped to talk" to the Matthews' caged monkey, and Marcia "gave cats to everyone," though she still seemed to have about thirty-seven cats on hand at all times. Many swam in the adobe pool, which Jason filled by attaching a six-inch pipe to an airplane engine and shooting water from a well fifteen feet through the air and into the pool.

Visitors admired the home's front doors, inspired by the doors of the Spanish Governor's Palace in San Antonio and crafted by master woodcarver Peter Mansbendel of Austin. The custom gargoyles and cherubs of the Matthews' doors featured likenesses of Jason, Marcia, and their two children. Many guests marveled as Jason pointed out the cedar beams in the home's corridor, explaining how the king of Lebanon presented them to him in gratitude for his service in the Arab Revolt of 1916–1918, which made Lawrence of Arabia famous. Others were fascinated by the hydroponic tomatoes and other experiments Jason conducted in his greenhouse. Some of the methods developed at Quinta Mazatlan were reportedly employed to feed soldiers in Guam during World War II.

Despite their active socializing, Jason and Marcia still seemed remote to other McAllen folks. "She went to everything in town," one said of Marcia, "a charming woman . . . interesting and well informed. A perfect lady . . . but not accepted by the community." Jason, the informant related, would often "go into meditation. A trance. Just looking off into space. You'd come in the room and he'd not even know you were there. Then in a little while he'd snap out of it."

"One day," recalled another McAllen resident, Jason "would be just as common as an old shoe. The next day you'd think he was the King of England the way he acted."

In 1947, according to one source, Jason went to Hollywood to work in the film industry, and when he returned to McAllen in 1949, he was convinced that the United Nations was a Communist front and that Western civilization was in an alarming decline. The couple's political views became even more conservative throughout the 1950s, and at some point they began publishing a magazine of political dialogue called *American Mercury*. (A magazine by the same name had been published much earlier by the noted pundit H. L. Mencken, but it is unclear whether there was any connection between the two publications.)

When an estate sale appraiser entered the home after Jason's death in 1964, he navigated narrow passageways bordered by high stacks of books, papers, and magazines. "Much of the furniture dates back to the eighteenth century, or earlier, and almost all of it qualifies as genuine antique," stated the *Monitor*, when announcing the sale in late September 1965. "The Matthews mixed periods and styles indiscriminately in their décor, giving an unusual and distinctive flavor." The sale also featured such items as a saber that Jason had reportedly seized while fighting with Pancho Villa in Mexico and a parrot that sang grand opera.

32

Four Great Ladies

MARY NEELY

Mary Neely didn't have a telephone in her home until 1987, just a year before she died at age 107. Her ranch on the Rio Grande, south of Sierra Blanca, was so remote that phone service had never been feasible until the Rural Electrification Administration obtained funding for a solar-powered microwave radio on a nearby hill that would carry signals to and from the house.

Born in Comanche in 1880, Mrs. Neely had come to West Texas in 1902 in a covered wagon. Like many remarkable women in that vast landscape, she never missed things like telephones in a time and place where a person had to deal with Pancho Villa, cattle rustlers, flash floods, panthers, and rattlesnakes.

By 1893, Mary's father, frontier doctor Frank Holmsley, had moved the family to Maverick in Runnels County. Shortly thereafter, her younger brother Tom was born in unusual circumstances even by pioneer standards. Earlier that day, Dr. Holmsley had lost part of an arm and injured his remaining hand in a cotton gin accident. As the only other doctor in the area was found stewed to the gills, Mary's father delivered Tom with one arm. (No worse the wear for it, Tom also made it to the century mark.)

At age thirteen, Mary became Dr. Holmsley's hands, helping him deliver babies, bind wounds, and mix and dole out medicines. After her marriage to Joe Neely and their westward trek to Hudspeth County, she used that experience to serve people on both sides of the Rio Grande as a midwife and medic. Far and wide, folks knew her as Grandma Neely.

In 1985, Governor Mark White proclaimed December 28, the date of her 105th birthday, as Mary Neely Day. "Her book-lined living room is a testament to her hunger to learn, whether from Einstein or Plato, Solzhenitsyn or Freud," the governor remarked. "Few of us will have the opportunity to live a life such as Mary's—one that has spanned a century and the most revolutionary changes in history."

"She was a philosopher," recalled the late Bill Hallman of Austin, who met Mary in 1986 and worked on a book about her life. "The growth and development of the soul, mind, and spirit of man fascinated her. She was bilingual *and* bicultural—she could write in an elegant style and round up the goats by cussing a cowboy blue streak."

EILEEN WINDSOR ALVES

The practice of archeology was still a young science in Texas when Eileen Windsor Alves (1873–1935) took to the field from her El Paso home in the 1920s. Driving her non-motorist husband, Burrow Alves, on his china and restaurant-supply sales trips around the Southwest, Eileen visited archeologists and conducted archeological work along the way.

The field trips resulted in the publication of papers and presentation of talks with titles such as "Shelter Caves of the El Paso District," "Pottery of the El Paso Region," "Perishable Artifacts of the Hueco Caves," and "Fetish Stones from Near El Paso." Eileen was an early campaigner against the destruction of sites by looters. As Carolyn O'Bagy Davis wrote in a 2000 issue of *The Artifact*, published by the El Paso Archaeological Society, Eileen purchased the collection of a hunter who had carried off relics from the site named Ceremonial Cave, near El Paso. The items included "darts with wood foreshafts, staffs, pendants, strings of beads, bits of basketry, a coiled basketry armband studded with turquoise mosaic, ceremonial staffs, hair ornaments, and painted *tablitas*." She donated the collection to an Arizona archive, and today many of the relics are housed at the University of Texas Archeological Research Library.

Creatures of the desert were another of Eileen's passions. She often gathered the critters when camping out on Burrow's sales trips. At one point, notes Carolyn O'Bagy Davis, the Alves' El Paso household pets included scorpions, a kangaroo rat, a huge desert tortoise, several alligators, snakes, and six Gila monsters. "There was a cage of owls in the office and three skunks," writes Davis, "one of which got loose and lived afterwards in the space under the house, venturing out at night to dig up her flowers and shrubs."

MARIA "CHATA" SADA

Maria "Chata" Sada ran a trading post, restaurant, and informal motel at Boquillas, just across the Rio Grande from the Mexican village of the same name, in the Big Bend before it became a national park. Born in Guanajuato in 1884, Chata married Juan Sada in 1901 in Boquillas, Mexico, where Juan owned a small silver mine. In 1906, she moved across the river, established her business, and carried on an international romance with her husband. Fort Worth reporter Presley Bryant wrote that Chata reigned as "the chatelaine of Boquillas, Texas, until the national park came into existence in 1944."

Food critic Duncan Hines reportedly recommended Chata's cuisine. Big Bend photographer W. D. Smithers spoke fondly of the twenty-five-cent meals as well. San Antonio scribbler Sam Woolford noted that Chata's Rio Grande outpost of adobe and peeled cottonwood logs "smelled of wet clay and watered-down dirt floors and fresh tortillas, and of the moonflowers that grew in the shade of the brush arbor out front." Chata's tortillas, wrote Sam, served on tablecloths of starched flour sacks, were "more pungent, someway, her tamales more drippy and a bit more fiery, her chili just a shade tastier than dishes served on linen with silver, in other establishments."

W. D. Smithers said Chata provided medicines to the area's less fortunate folks; she "served as midwife, and acted as priest, judge, and teacher." After Juan died and Big Bend National Park opened in 1944, Chata moved to Del Rio to live with one of the many orphans the couple had raised.

ADA ELLIOTT

Few men or women in the state managed to squeeze as much living into a long life as Ada Elliott. Born sometime after 1888, she moved with her family from Arkansas to Waco in 1900. Five years later she was performing across the South with a vaudeville troupe. In 1907, she attended Baylor, where she organized a protest to allow a socialist (who was also a past Baylor president) to speak on campus. After a year of college, she taught for a year at Bugscuffle, twenty miles northwest of Waco.

Later, Ada lived in the oil boomtown of Desdemona, also called Hog Town, where she published the *Desdemona Oil News* with her husband, the town mayor. She also found time to travel the state by train, horse, and buggy, stumping for suffrage. Once, when giving "some kind of civil rights talk," as she recalled to a reporter in 1978, a woman in the audience objected to something Ada had said, rushed to the podium, and slapped her. "I grabbed her hair, and we really went at it," said Ada.

Reportedly, Ada once found herself gambling in a Nogales, Mexico, cantina while Pancho Villa tried his luck at a nearby table. In the 1930s, she acted on Broadway, appearing in *Three Men on a Horse, Blind Alley, Evening Star,* and other shows. In her later years, with a corncob pipe in one hand, Ada took up a pen in the other. Her 1977 book, *801: Beans, Potatoes, and Apple Pie,* covers the days when she ran a boardinghouse in Dallas. In 1978, the year of her last known interview, she was working on two other books, *First Lady of Hogtown,* about her Desdemona days, and *Hypnosis Opened the Door to Strange Psychic Powers,* about her experience with medical hypnosis.

33

Five Aces of Magic

PROFESSOR PEARL REYNOLDS

Publicity for nineteenth-century Texas magician Professor Pearl Reynolds promised a "Death-Defying Act!" Traveling from town to town in a painted, horse-drawn wagon, the "Master of Illusion" would ascend in a hot air balloon to promote an upcoming performance. Onlookers gasped as the professor leapt from the balloon's basket, opened a parachute, and floated to earth, according to a report by the Texas Association of Magicians. Few townsfolk could then resist Reynolds' invitation to attend that evening's presentation of Oriental magic and other mysteries.

WILLARD THE WIZARD

The Texas Association of Magicians' Royal Order of Willard (which honors twenty-five-year members) pays tribute to the legendary Texas tent-show magician Harry Willard, better known as Willard the Wizard. Harry came from a long line of family magicians—each billed

Willard the Wizard mesmerizes a rooster, circa 1941. Courtesy of the *San Antonio Light* Collection, Institute of Texan Cultures, No. L-2691-A, courtesy of the Hearst Corporation.

as Willard the Wizard—stretching back to the 1840s in Ireland. Born while the family was performing in Clarksville in 1895, Harry later toured for decades from a home base in San Antonio. An undated clipping for a performance in Llano states that the Wizard would shoot a man from a cannon into a nest of trunks suspended from the tent's center pole and perform such mysteries as "the decapitated princess, the disappearing automobile, the Hindoo rope mystery, and his sensational escape from a steel boiler tank after being welded in the tank by the best local welders." Magician Bev Bergeron, author of the 1978 book *Willard the Wizard*, says that Harry Willard "startled the world with his thumb tie and his Spirit Cabinet."

DITTMANN

As a young man, Texas movie pioneer Adolf Dittmann thrilled audiences across the nation with his artful legerdemain. In Chicago, the magician owned the Dittmann Publishing House, where he wrote and published songs. In 1907, a visit to the Rio Grande Valley so impressed the versatile showman that he decided to move there permanently.

After settling in Brownsville in 1908, Dittmann bought the old Teatro Electrico, or Electric Theater, where he presented vaudeville shows and silent films. In his spare time he worked as a freelance photographer for Pathe News Service. In 1910, he built Brownsville's first real movie house, the Dittmann Theater.

That same year, the Mexican Revolution began in western Chihuahua. As various factions, led by Emiliano Zapata, Pancho Villa, Venustiano Carranza, and others, battled throughout Mexico, Dittmann decided to provide footage of the revolution to newsreel services.

In May 1913, Dittmann, local attorney and historian Frank Pierce, and *Brownsville Herald* editor Mose Stein sought out *Carrancista* rebels in Matamoros. "We didn't know how we'd be received—with the fatted calf or with a firing squad at sunrise," Dittmann told a reporter years later. But the trio's fears soon dissipated. General Lucio Blanco welcomed the Americans to lunch at his camp, paraded his men in front of the camera, and responded affably to Stein's interview questions. Pierce collected mental notes that would appear four years later in his book *Texas' Last Frontier: A Brief History of the Lower Rio Grande Valley of Texas.*

A few days later, as Blanco's army attacked Matamoros, Dittmann captured the siege on movie film and developed it in the basement of his theater. "I shot the stuff one day and had it on the screen the next," he recalled in 1944. Released under the company name of Dittmann's Moving Pictures, *The Battle of Matamoros* was shown throughout the Southwest.

Today, the Historic Brownsville Museum exhibits Adolf Dittmann's hand-cranked camera and some of the one-time prestidigitator's magic paraphernalia.

HERMAN YERGER

In the mid-1940s, Austin magician Herman Yerger held magical get-togethers that evolved into the Texas Association of Magicians. At the time, Yerger ran an alternative pharmacy at 1011 Red River Street in Austin that sold home remedies, herbs, and such tonics and potions as High John the Conqueror root. With a crystal ball, he told folks' fortunes.

Born in Brooklyn in 1894, Herman operated a tent show for a time with his wife Emile, selling tonics and doing a little magic. "He would bury a person alive as part of the show," says Austin magician Ramon Galindo, who calls Yerger his mentor.

By the 1940s, Herman was in a wheelchair—the result of a fall years before while working as a tightwire walker, according to some stories. Others said a knife attack had left a shard of blade in his spine. "I refuse to admit," Yerger wrote, with the positive perception of one accustomed to making the impossible possible, "that my physical defects are overwhelming. They are something to be lived with, compromised with, and conquered."

"Herman was a good performer," observed Texas magic historian Claude Crowe, "with an aura of mysterioso."

O'QUINN CAIRO III

While playing trumpet in Austin's Tillotson College (now Huston-Tillotson) orchestra in the 1940s, O'Quinn Cairo III distinguished himself by wearing glove puppets and light-up bow ties. He later led a twenty-piece swing band on tours of the Southwest.

Born in Manor in 1923, O'Quinn first experienced the thrill of pres-

tidigitation at age eight, when he witnessed a Herman Yerger performance. Soon, he was mastering tricks ordered from ads in comic books,
and the experience helped him deal with the grief of his father's early
death.

Around 1960, O'Quinn became the first black member of the Texas
Association of Magicians. "Without the international brotherhood feeling among magicians, I would not be a magician today," he stated in
1986. "They accepted me as a magician, not a color."

34

Mystics

"There Is No Death"

Some residents of the state find it such a paradise that they become
exceedingly reluctant to continue their journey to the realm beyond.
In 1930, for instance, press reports noted that a Rio Grande City
woman, Laura Lara, claimed to be 140 years old. She had been a grand-
mother during the Mexican War, the story went, and had served as
Robert E. Lee's laundress when he was stationed at Fort Ringgold. Dallas oilman H. L. Hunt sought to break the purported world's record for
longevity—167 years—but left this world a mere whippersnapper at
eighty-five. In 1999, when Houston geophysicist Miller Quarles was
eighty-five, a BBC program reported that Quarles "offered a fortune to
anyone who can prevent him from dying." Founder of the Curing Old
Age Disease Society, Quarles financed scientific research in the hopes of
being cloned, but in 2000 he reportedly withdrew his offer of a cash
reward for immortality.

Perhaps Quarles, who appears to still be with us as of early 2006, has
adopted the views of many nineteenth-century Texans: that eternal life,
or at least an eternal hotline to this life, is already a done deal if we mortals only mind our manners. The religious philosophy of "Modern Spir-
itualism" spread across the country in 1848, when two sisters in New

York state convinced people that they had begun receiving "spirit messages" from the dead. The metaphysical fad reached Texas at least by the 1870s, when the monthly magazine the *Texas Spiritualist* began publication at Hempstead. "There is no death," proclaimed the front page of every issue. "The works of nature declare the fact of everlasting life."

One issue of the magazine carried a phrenological chart for Waller County schoolteacher Colonel William L. Booth, who was deemed "well qualified" for his position as president of the Spiritual and Liberal Association of Texas. (Phrenology is based on the belief that character traits and mental abilities can be assessed by examining the configuration of a person's skull.) Another magazine called the *Harmonia*, published in Waco during the 1880s, featured "spirit communications" received by medium Mrs. Alice Black.

During the same period, railroad builder Paul Bremond formed a Spiritualist society in Houston. Bremond credited spiritual guidance channeled from Moseley Baker, a deceased veteran of the Battle of San Jacinto, for directing his construction of the Houston, East, and West Texas Railroad in the 1870s.

In 1927, as many as two thousand Spiritualists from all over the country materialized in San Antonio for the thirty-fifth annual convention of the National Spiritualist Association. A party of fifty Comanches, in town for the Old Trail Drivers Reunion, visited the convention at the Gunter Hotel. The Indians, reported the *San Antonio Express*, delivered "a request to communicate with departed tribal chieftains." The paper did not say whether a connection was made.

JIMMIE AND BELLE SHRUM: SEEING WITH EYES WIDE SHUT

Medical folklore holds that a baby born with a caul—a part of the embryonic membrane that sometimes covers the head at birth—might possess uncommon intuitive powers, perhaps even clairvoyance or "second sight."

When Jimmie and Belle Shrum were born (probably in Comanche County, where the family was living a few years later), in 1880 and 1882, respectively, they entered the world "with a veil over their faces," as their mother described the condition. The other eight Shrum children were born normally. "The old doctor who brought Belle into the world said that if she lived," wrote Mary Whatley Clarke in her 1956 book, *The Palo Pinto Story*, "she would be gifted with second sight."

Jimmie's abilities became known one night when Mr. Shrum was late returning to Comanche County from Brownwood. The boy closed his eyes and pressed his hands over them, then—to his mother's eventual astonishment—described exactly the circumstances of his father's delay. When little Belle's knack for "seeing" became known, and rumors circulated of the two children's "queer doings," the family moved three counties over, to Johnson County.

After Belle "saw" the location of a lost little brother at a camp meeting in Burleson, and word spread again, the Shrums moved to Eastland County, where a Dr. Gilbert of Ranger became very interested in the children's uncanny abilities. In 1894, he took them to the State Fair, where a *Dallas Morning News* article described them as "diminutive prodigies" who performed "feats of the telepathic order."

Later, living in Mineral Wells, Belle and Jimmie went on tour, demonstrating their abilities in other Texas towns and as far away as Tennessee and Arizona.

Society Psychic

When Wilhelmina Von Abee Sckerls, the widow of San Antonio business and civic leader Charles Adolph Sckerls, died in 1928 at age sixty-seven, the *San Antonio Light* observed that she possessed "a psychic sense which was developed to a high degree," and that "for many years she was advisor and counselor to many prominent San Antonio businessmen."

Friend and pallbearer Joseph P. Devine observed, "Thousands of persons in all walks of life, from the humblest to the greatest . . . will feel a sense of personal loss in the passing of this frail little woman, who has rendered unforgettable service to more individuals than any other single San Antonian."

"Madam Sckerls, as she was better known, was a striking example of the wearing away of the physical by the dominance of the spiritual attained on behalf of others. Her death in the main was attributed to this fact," reported the *New Encyclopedia of Texas*. "Her psychic power became known when she was a young housewife and mother in the midst of her community, on Madison Street . . . Her influence widened until . . . her home was besieged by those who came to her with their problems and troubles, and her noble heart was open always to those in distress . . . From the earliest manifestation of her psychic powers, as a young girl in her native Germany, she recognized it as a divinely implanted gift and steadfastly refused to commercialize it."

METAPHYSICS IN THE OIL FIELDS

In their efforts to predict which patches of earth might yield liquid gold, Texas wildcatters tried everything under the sun, including consulting clairvoyants. Stories of mystical geology abound in oil lore.

Born in Mexia in 1893, a black psychic named Annie Jackson reportedly located a gusher for J. K. Hughes around 1918, after instructing him that his first choice for a drilling site would not yield oil. Years later, as Alva Taylor wrote in *Taylor's History and Photographs of Corsicana and Navarro County* (1959), Hughes "wanted to see if Annie knew what she was talking about" and drilled a dry hole at the first location. She also found oil for Colonel A. E. Humphreys, the wildcatter who drilled what is regarded as the discovery well of the Mexia field in 1920. Humphreys rewarded her with some $8,500, with which Annie built a large home in Corsicana. There, she attracted a steady stream of folks from all walks of life, who came to her for faith healing and advice on a wide range of subjects. Her clients even included a future Texas governor, Beauford Jester.

When writer and folklorist William A. Owens visited the "Seer of Corsicana" in 1956 to record an interview with her for the University of Texas Oral History of Texas Oil Pioneers project, he found an integrated waiting room crowded with steadfast believers from all over the state. Though she mixed clairvoyant prophecy with Christian testimony and shouting holy-ghost gospel performances, Annie insisted on proper decorum. A sign informed clients: "I will not read to 'women' who 'smoke' are ware 'pants' are 'slacks' here. Positively no 'drinking.' By Mrs. Annie Jackson."

Owens described Annie as "remarkably well-preserved for the sixty-three years she claims. Her skin is soft dark brown, her eyes dark, emotional, with a look that seems to pierce ordinary barriers. She was wearing a gray faille suit, pale gold silk blouse, and brown velvet pumps with high heels." When Owens asked her when she started giving advice, Annie replied, "All my life—I born that way." She related that her mother had apparently been unaware that she was pregnant until the woman for whom she worked asked if she was "fixin' to born a baby this mornin'." By the time a doctor came from Groesbeck, Annie had arrived.

> The doctor come in and says, "I love fresh meat." Says, "You all done killed hogs?" Said, "Here's a nice hog heart, hog lights, and chitlin's." White lady say, "No, that's Aunt Margret's baby." "Aunt Margret's baby!" Says, "Well, I ain't never seen anythin' like that." . . . And so when he examined me, my feet was back that a'way and my arms [unintelligible]. My head kinda knocked my shoulder. He says, "Look a'here. She got a mouth full of teeth." Says, "Aunt Margret," says, "This is a clairvayan." Says, "What is a clairvayan, Doctor?" Says, "Some of them calls them fortune-tellers. She's no fortune-teller." Says, "She goin' tell you things under the earth jus' like she can on top."

Though some of the advice Annie provided her clients could have been described by the broadly-applied term "fortune-telling," her psychic reading method was unique. When Owens asked how people knew about her work, she replied,

> How do they know? 'Cause of me sittin' down and tellin' 'em the truth. See, I tells so much truth in there—the future and the past—the future and the past—all it is, the future and past. That's all people got in this world, jus' future and past. Yo' life—yo' palm, yo' blood circle into yo' blood. See, I reads by blood circlin'—yo' blood circlin'. It's not yo' lines or nothin', it's yo' blood that carries to the palms of yo' hand and through yo' skin. That's the way it goes.

A psychic named Ruth Bryan, who used the professional name of Madame Virginia, added her voice to the oral history of the Texas oil industry in 1959, interviewed in Abilene by Robert A. Montgomery.

After locating oil in the Burkburnett field, Madame Virginia became sought-after by wildcatters. "It just comes to me," she explained of her ability.

> It just comes to me. A reader has a seeing mind just like other people has seeing eyes. It taken me years to learn this. And I can see better with my mind than I can see with my eyes. And if I'm talking to someone about a plot of land and they go to draw me a plot of their land, I stop them, because I can't see the same with my eyes as I see with my mind.

Madame Virginia explained that she could ride in a train and perceive when the train was passing over land that contained oil. When an East Texas well mysteriously played out, the oilmen asked her what she thought. "And in looking at this oil," Madame Virginia recalled, "it looked like an underground, dark underground river . . . like it went like a waterfall. It had fell, just like a waterfall." She advised the men to drill deeper, and they found more oil in three different strata of sands.

Around the turn of the century, an oil-locator in the Uvalde area, Guy M. Finley, became famous as "the boy with the x-ray eyes" after he repeatedly found groundwater. Shortly after the Spindletop gusher in 1901, hopeful investors took thirteen-year-old Guy to the boomtown south of Beaumont. Legend says that the young petro-prophet did locate some oil at Spindletop. As Finley described it, he couldn't actually see into the ground, but would have "a sort of vision." But in 1965, Finley told writer Frank X. Tolbert that the commercialization of his unusual powers had caused them to wane. They returned somewhat in later years, and he often located water for people free of charge.

"Old-timers will recall that the oil country was infested with oil smellers," recalled another oilman for the University of Texas Oral History of Texas Oil Pioneers project.

> One prominent Texas preacher went so far as to allege that he had x-ray eyes. He was a dramatist of the very highest order. His acting was superb, he would hold his hands high over his head as though he was pointing to the heavenly bodies, and with closed eyes would majestically prance

135

around—suddenly stop, shudder as though he had palsy, and in a centurian voice would declare that he was on the edge of an oil creek that was narrow, about fifty feet wide, and the main oil river would be found in the immediate vicinity. He was the most impressive of all the oil-smellers I have ever met, and should have quit the oil-smelling business, and gone on the stage . . . He was operating out of Petrolia. Another oil smeller had a small black box, and a comb-shaped instrument which he alleged had been entrusted to him by a life prisoner in a Spanish dungeon. Believe it or not, this oil smeller had the financial support of a wealthy and prominent Dallas businessman.

EDGAR AND EDGAR

Theosophy student and recent engineering graduate Morris O. Rayor shouldn't have felt bad when the séances he held around Luling in the mid-1910s failed to provide data from the spirit world on Caldwell County oil reservoirs. In 1921, one of the most famous metaphysicians in American history also missed the big strike. With its headquarters in Cleburne, the Edgar Cayce Petroleum Company hoped for a successful well that would fund Cayce's hospital of psychic healing. But even though the trance readings conducted in Cleburne instructed Cayce and associates to drill at the oil-rich outskirts of Luling and Desdemona, they never found the underground river of gold.

Discovery of the great Luling field was left to another Edgar with a serious interest in the spiritual side of life. A native of Brockton, Massachusetts, who had already made and given away a fortune in the rubber industry, Edgar B. Davis struck his gusher in 1922. Guided by intuition and a remarkably steadfast faith, Davis—against the advice of most geological experts—pioneered oil production in the Edwards lime and Austin chalk formations. As biographer Riley Froh notes in *Edgar B. Davis: Wildcatter Extraordinary* (1984) and *Edgar B. Davis and Sequences of Business Capitalism* (1993), one of the oilman's "most deeply rooted characteristics . . . his self-confidence, sprung from his Calvinism: the greater the struggle, the greater the reward." Such a philosophy, of course, would come in handy for any wildcatter rolling the dice against all odds.

Feeling that his gushers were gifts from the Almighty, the oilman also pioneered capitalist profit sharing and redistributed his worldly bounty to such a degree that one associate considered him "visionary and impractical." In 1936, a duo of rubber industry historians described Edgar B. as "one share-the-wealth messiah who actually has practiced what he preaches," in an apparent reference to the charitable pontifications of Huey Long. The duo further opined that the Texas Yankee had become "renowned for carrying generosity to the limits of eccentricity." After selling his Luling properties to Magnolia Petroleum Company in 1926 for twelve million dollars, Edgar B. went on a sharing spree of amazing proportion. "I may go broke again," Riley Froh credits the oilman as saying at the time, "but it looks as though I would have the fun of giving away several millions of dollars before I do so."

First, Riley writes, Davis threw "the world's biggest free picnic" on June 5, 1926. Some one hundred acres south of Luling, along the San Marcos River, hosted at least fifteen thousand folks. "It was so well attended," Froh notes, "that when parking space ran out along the river, Davis quickly purchased an adjacent field, and late arrivals drove out on the corn crop." The picnickers consumed "12,200 pounds of beef, 5,180 pounds of mutton, 2,000 fryers, 8,700 ice cream sandwiches, 85 gallons of ice cream, 7,000 cakes, 6,560 bottles of near beer, 28,800 bottles of soft drinks, and unknown quantities of beans, potato salad, pickles, and coffee."

Though Davis held progressive racial views for the era, he sponsored a separate picnic for blacks north of Luling, where attendees enjoyed a performance by an all-black jazz band from San Antonio. The Alamo City Municipal Band played for the white picnic, and both gatherings enjoyed a concert by three New York opera stars Davis imported for the event. "Then," Riley continues, "the guests settled down to light up 7,500 cigars and 100,000 cigarettes while Davis described his scheme of philanthropy, charity, and almsgiving."

In addition to his liberal bonuses and profit-sharing, Edgar B. announced that he would turn the picnic site into a community park, complete with a club house, golf course, and other recreational facilities. He also revealed plans for an eighty-acre park for the black community and for a model farm where agricultural research would be conducted to benefit area farmers. And he continued vigorous giving to a number of causes for the next three years.

His zestful love of the arts inspired much of his patronage. In the late 1920s, the oilman sponsored several years of wildflower painting competitions in San Antonio. Many of the finest works produced in this milestone event for Texas art and artists are reproduced in William E. Reeves Jr.'s 1998 book, *Texas Art and a Wildcatter's Dream*. Another philanthropic venture, the production of a Broadway play, afforded Davis the opportunity to combine an appreciation of theatre with his mystical interests. Edgar B. commissioned San Antonio author J. Frank Davis (no relation) to write a drama about reincarnation entitled *The Ladder*. When the show opened in 1926, New York critics blasted the production to smithereens. Alexander Woolcott, for instance, deemed *The Ladder* "a large, richly upholstered piece of nothing at all." Attendance remained slim until Davis suspended admission fees and began awarding cash prizes for essays on the play. As Riley Froh explains, by the time the show closed in 1928, the wildcatter had spent $1.2 million on it. J. Frank Davis recovered from his "critical wounds" to become supervisor of the Works Progress Administration's Texas Writers' Project in the 1930s. Edgar Cayce attended a performance of *The Ladder* in New York, and the two Edgars met again in the late 1930s, when Davis came to Cayce hoping to resolve business conflicts over the merger of two giant rubber corporations by having Cayce perform a trance reading.

Though he generally spoke of the experience to only his most intimate associates, Edgar B. Davis might also have asked Edgar Cayce about a mystical voice that spoke to him in 1904, informing Davis that he was destined to become president of the United States. Prior to the 1928 National Democratic Convention in Houston, a Pulitzer Prize–winning journalist boosted Davis as an ideal vice-presidential candidate to share the ticket with Al Smith. But as Riley Froh points out, Davis himself pursued the nomination in the most passive fashion imaginable, and then of course there was the fact that "the oilman had squandered a million dollars on a bad play—an eccentricity not attractive to conservative politics."

Nonetheless, Davis never dismissed the prophecy of 1904. His great wealth long given away, for several years before his death in 1951, he poured his all into an unsuccessful well at Buckeye in Matagorda

County. Somehow, the man of faith intuited, a roaring gusher at Buckeye would lead to his election to the highest office in the land.

After his passing, scribblers and oil field veterans continued spreading Edgar B. legends and lore for decades. Some folks, for instance, whoppered that Davis chose to drill his wells at fields that boasted the prettiest wildflowers. But as his biographer adeptly demonstrates, the mystic from Massachusetts was one Texas maverick who was "not only stranger than the fiction about him" but also "more interesting."

APPENDIXES

INTRODUCTION

My perspective on performance art as a framework for viewing a wide range of human behavior is formed not only by study and observation but also by participation in the medium. I began performing and writing for theatre during the Johnson administration, and while much of my work could be considered relatively traditional playwriting—or somewhat traditionally experimental playwriting—some of my work seemed to function in the cross-discipline format of performance. (The piece *Western Art*, for example, is performed as a kind of puppet show with several-inch-high plastic western figures and is intended as a cartoon commentary on certain aspects of contemporary art theory.) The appendixes that follow offer a sampling of that work.

The Zeb Crawburg Memorial

"Living sculpture" has long been an important component of performance art.

In 1929, Greenville, Texas, hosted a stunning work of performance folk-art during dedication ceremonies for the new Hunt County Courthouse. After orators praised the structure and children sang the state song, the crowd of thousands hushed as living statuary appeared on the narrow outer ledge of the courthouse's third floor. Five costumed figures stood in a dramatic tableau depicting "Justice," "Pioneer Woman," "Pioneer Man," "Texas Ranger," and "Cowboy."

Living sculpture performance at the Hunt County Courthouse dedication, circa 1929. Courtesy of the Northeast Texas History and Genealogy Center, W. Walworth Harrison Public Library, Greenville, Texas.

APPENDIX A

The 1929 work of performance folk-art got a rave review in 1996, when Hunt County applied for Texas Historic Landmark status for its temple of justice. "We'd sent the State Historical Commission photos of the courthouse both with and without the living statuary," explained county historian Carol Taylor. "The commission thought we'd altered the building by removing the statues and almost denied our request for a marker. They thought the people were real statues!"

In a similar tradition, I enacted a living statuary performance in Austin in October 1978. The *Zeb Crawburg Memorial* was performed under a portico on the front lawn of the Elisabet Ney Museum, a building that once served as the studio of sculptor Elisabet Ney (1833–1907). Born in Germany and educated in the school of classical naturalism as the first woman to attend the Munich Art Academy, Elisabet moved to America after the outbreak of the Franco-Prussian War in 1870, eventually settling in Central Texas. During her career she made sculptures of figures such as Bismarck, Garibaldi, Jacob Grimm, Schopenhauer, Ludwig II of Bavaria, Lady Macbeth, Stephen F. Austin, Sam Houston, and many oth-

The *Zeb Crawburg Memorial*. Photos by Jim Fisher.

ers. The studio, built in the 1890s, is open to the public and continuously exhibits art work and artifacts from the life of Elisabet Ney.

I portrayed a statue of a fictitious nineteenth-century western figure named Zeb Crawburg. Several persons were invited to be present on a panel as bogus historians and to give lectures on Zeb's significance in Texas and American history and on the origin of the sculpture itself. I wore a faded black cowboy hat, black antique western gunslinger cloak, real-looking toy six-shooters and holsters, black western shirt and pants, and dusty boots.

The performance lasted almost an hour, during which the historians presented a wide range of unusual interpretations of Crawburg's life and career. I struggled to remain perfectly still and to keep from laughing at their bizarre theories and eccentric professorial deliveries. At all times I tried to appear historically monumental, imbued with the profound horizon-searching gaze and visionary demeanor characteristic of the sculptural interpretations of frontier personalities. The historians argued and professionally insulted one another, each insisting that he or she had unearthed Zeb Crawburg's true story. Endless detail and Crawburgian minutiae spouted forth, accompanied in the case of one particularly nervous historian by the frequent and abrupt refrain, "But that's the subject of another paper."

The *Zeb Crawburg Memorial* was viewed by a small invited audience, as well as many people who were visiting the museum that day to view Elisabet Ney's sculpture. I was told later that some of them appeared to believe they were witnessing some kind of highly serious, official ceremony and moved around the perimeters of the performance area in a hushed, respectful manner. Others were puzzled and curious and stopped to observe. And some made tourist-style snapshots, which leads me to hope that the piece has been documented in family photo albums of folks I'll never meet.

• • •

The *Zeb Crawburg Memorial* appeared in the March 1979 issue of *High Performance*, Los Angeles.

AstroTurf Ranchette

SOUND. An audio tape plays a narrative, spoken in a thick Texas accent, about a couple in a 1957 Chevy driving out to West Texas. The narrator tells us that he moved to Houston two years ago from the Northeast because his father is in the oil business. In order to discover the "real" Texas, they acquired business interests around the state—a maternity shop in Nacogdoches, resort condominiums in Terlingua, etc. The narrator and a woman named Sheila are driving out to West Texas to check on a subdivision called the AstroTurf Ranchettes: two acre ranches with AstroTurf lawns for easy maintenance. As they enter a winding Trans-Pecos canyon, they come upon several giant western figures, standing

AstroTurf Ranchette. Photo by Stuart Heady.

frozen in time. Sheila compares them to icons. The narrator parks the Chevy and they gaze in historical rapture at the figures until the sun goes down, when "I slipped the little '57 into gear and headed on out to the AstroTurf Ranchette. And as the sun began to sink slowly in the West, I heard music."

ACTION. There are several six-inch-high brightly colored plastic western figures on the ground. I am dressed in black gunfighter clothing. As the tape plays I crawl on the ground, moving a red model '57 Chevy along, imagining it passing through the Trans-Pecos landscape. When the narrator describes the arrival at the canyon of the giant western figures, the model '57 arrives at the plastic western figures. After the Chevy departs, I play a strain of "Red River Valley" on a baritone horn.

• • •

AstroTurf Ranchette was performed between 1979 and 1982 at the Elisabet Ney Museum, Trinity House Gallery, Laundry Lounge, Nierika Studio, Dougherty Cultural Arts Center, and the Austin Museum of Art–Laguna Gloria, all in Austin; Downtown Center for the Arts, Albuquerque; Randolph Street Gallery, Chicago; the Mattress Factory, Pittsburgh; and the Dallas Arts Festival. The piece appeared in the summer 1981 issue of *Artspace*, Albuquerque.

Appendix C

Western Art

Two western artists, Mondo and Vegas, portrayed by small plastic cowboy figures, enter firing wildly. Mondo speaks in a grizzly western drawl, Vegas in a much milder western drawl.

VEGAS. Mondo. Mondo. You hit?

MONDO. Naw, naw. Old Indian trick. Move like a shadow. Don't get hit. Wiped out them bushwhackers though. Short order.

VEGAS. Good shooting, Mondo. Excellent performance. Flawless technique. Dazzling finger action.

MONDO. Aw, it's nothin' . . . Say, Vegas?

VEGAS. Yeah?

MONDO. Vegas, I don't mean to complain or nothin', but I was wonderin' when we was gonna pull off some real capers.

VEGAS. Your commission's not high enough? You wanna raise?

MONDO. Naw, naw, the dough's fine. It's jes' that—well we been doin' these pretend type rehearsal jobs so long I'm afraid I might be gettin' rusty. I need the real stuff, Vegas. Real guns an' real banks an' real cops an' liquor stores an' stuff.

VEGAS. Risky. Risky. Much too risky, Mondo. The perfect outlaw never does anything he might get caught doin'.

MONDO. Yeah but if you don't never do nothin' you're not a real outlaw.

VEGAS. It's the idea of the crime, Mondo. The idea is so much nobler than the act itself. Conceptual crime is so much more subversive and thrilling than physical, object-based reality.

MONDO. That still don't do nothin' 'bout the jumpy feelin' I get in my guts, Vegas. I need some real action, with real screams an' real terror— I need the real stuff.

VEGAS. What about that museum heist we pulled in D.C.? You fired wild into the crowd. I've never seen such panic.

MONDO. Blanks, man, we was usin' blanks.

VEGAS. Yeah, but they still handed over that fat check just as pretty as you please. And we got some pretty good reviews, too.

MONDO. Nobody reads that amusement page stuff, Vegas. We need some front page action. Headlines. Big, thick, black letters with grainy on-the-scene photos.

VEGAS. You're talkin' chain gang now, Mondo.

MONDO. But Vegas—

VEGAS. You're talkin' bounty hunters, psycho sheriffs, stretched necks danglin' from nooses on the plaza at sundown.

MONDO. But Vegas—

VEGAS. You're talkin' installations in the stone walls down Laredo way. Throw away the key and—no documentation.

MONDO. But I been treadin' this line my whole dang career, Vegas. I feel myself, alive in space an' action, goin' around, goin' through the motions but—nothin's happenin'!

VEGAS. Mondo. Mondo. You remember all those reruns? *Gunsmoke. Rawhide. Have Gun Will Travel.* In the last five minutes of the show you're always holed up in some hovel somewhere and the hero comes along all of a sudden and leaves you fulla silver, lyin' in the middle of the desert. Is that what you want for an ontological model of reality? Every time you see one a them things you get so depressed you can't even don a bandana.

MONDO. Well, none a them outfits uses real guns neither. Jes' this stupid ol' plastic stuff. No wonder them laws always cut me down. Don't even let a man pack a real shootin' iron.

VEGAS. Get a grip on yourself, Mondo. Your picture once appeared in *TV Guide*! Aesthetic barometer of millions. Put it in perspective, pardner. Art. And life. Shove it into focus.

MONDO. I—I gotta rob me a stagecoach! A few big jobs, then disappear down Mexico way. Live out my days the easy way with all them pretty señoritas.

VEGAS. Mondo, I'm handin' you a European tour on a silver platter. Documenta. Festival d'Automne.

MONDO. Dynamite a train track!

VEGAS. A major retrospective at the Museum of Modern Art in Jerome, Arizona.

MONDO. No posse in the territory can track me down. My whiskers know the best hideouts on the back trails of the badlands.

VEGAS. Big thick catalogs with all your wanted posters flawlessly reproduced in chronological order. A critical summation of your notori-

ous career. Eyewitness narratives as testimony to your romantic outlaw inscrutability.

MONDO. I don't want none a that stuff! Mondo, I'm runnin' this gang
now. We're gonna ride into town tomorrow and take the bank. Either
you're with us or you ain't.

VEGAS. Good grief, Mondo. No need to overdramatize. You could just
put it on the expense account. Come on. Let's go back to the hotel
and watch *Laramie*. (*Exits*)

MONDO. Mondo Grubdoo. Wanted Dead or Alive. Killer of Twenty-four
Men. Most Feared Gun in the Territory. Wanted Dead or Alive.
Mondo Grubdoo. (*Looks around nervously, exits*)

• • •

Western Art was performed between 1979 and 1983 at the Austin Museum of
Art–Laguna Gloria, Trinity House Gallery, Dougherty Cultural Arts Center, and the
Texas Sculpture Symposium, all in Austin; Downtown Center for the Arts, Albu-
querque; Farmers Branch Public Library, Farmers Branch, Texas; Randolph Street
Gallery, Chicago; The Mattress Factory, Pittsburgh; and the Dallas Arts Festival. The
piece was published in the 1983 issue of *Cream City Review*, Milwaukee.

Break on Through

Ritual performance serves many purposes for humankind. As a mechanism for coping with adolescence and other life changes, in my early teens I engaged in a series of what I would call abstract expressionist psychodrama. I would mark out a space in a room or hallway and commence a period of flailing, thrashing, and wailing. And I recall clearly that when I returned from one of these fits, I felt as though I were in a new place, as if I had actually traveled in some way and had been fortified by the journey. The inconsistencies in and around me seemed a bit less maddening somehow after the purge.

These same drives, urges, and methods showed up later in two of my performance pieces. The first, *Let Them Take Up Serpents*, was performed in 1975 at the Contemporary Arts Museum in Houston and at the Zachary Scott Theater in Austin. It was originally conceived as a "hardcore journalism nerve drama" designed to simulate a religious snake-handling service as practiced by fundamentalist sects in the American South and was essentially represented as such in performance.

But in the actual physical reality of the piece, it became another kind of catalyst. While acting the role of the fervid, raving preacher, I found myself tapped into the same intense symbiosis of ecstasy and anguish that I experienced in my teenage ritual practice.

The piece began with a hymn delivered by a member of the congregation. Then the preacher mostly improvised a sermon which led to the appearance and dispensing of the "snakes." The singer collapsed upon receiving the snakes and began to thrash and flop about on the floor in a brutal, hysterical state of rapturous agony. A guitar player hopped across the stage, banging his guitar and emitting an eerie stream of rapid, choppy glossolalia. The preacher leapt and sprang through the arena, testifying in a furiously energetic state of disturbed frenzy. Other performers positioned throughout the audience read aloud factual accounts of deaths by snakebites incurred during services. The piece erupted for five to ten minutes and then seemed to end by some innate emotional gauge of its own.

The performers enacted a self-projection, entering a structure and

Let Them Take Up Serpents. Photo by Rodney K. Florence.

then surging through it, in an apparent effort to recover or discover some part of themselves. They sought to go somewhere, find something out, shock themselves and the congregation out of complacency by self-inducing a primal intensity.

The second piece, *Defense of the Nervous Breakdown as a Unification Technique*, was performed in 1976 at an alternative space called chURch in East Austin (as of 2007, the building has once again been converted to a church). I recorded a poem which projected the speaker's anxiety and his designs to break out of it physically. In performance, I played the tape and started with the exploration of corresponding, quasi-mimetic gestures and actions as an initial framework. As I then became possessed by the turbulence of the enactment, choreographic and emotional furiousness transcended any preconceived bounds or structure. I whirled and contorted and flung myself to the ground. I thrust upwards and ran and hurled my body full force into the wall, surprisingly without pain. I shivered and trembled with an intensity that startled and surprised me and presented new resources of strength, as the danger of psychic or physical violence gave way to a healthy, vigorous feeling of replenishment.

• • •

An earlier version of this essay appeared in the winter 1977 issue of *Artspace*, Albuquerque.

APPENDIX E

Zaney Blaney and the Beat

P ondering the roots of my long-held interest in the eccentric personality, it occurs to me that my father in particular seems to have been
something of a role model in that department. While his quirkiness
may not have risen to the operatic heights of some of the folks profiled
in these pages, certain of his obsessive-compulsive behaviors were
nonetheless anthropologically intriguing to a youngster. There was, for
instance, the constant ritual my friends called the Beat. As a professional
trumpet man and leader of his own big band, rhythm flowed out of the
man's body, seemingly beyond his control. Whenever he came home, no
matter the hour, the Beat became audible at the front door as he
pumped the key in and out *chk chukka chk chukka chk chukka chk* and so
on until the rhythm worked itself out long enough to allow him to pro-
ceed. Then it was coins and other items on the dresser top *tap tap tap
tappa tap tappa tap tappa tap taptaptap* until he at last felt the gods of the
Beat had been sufficiently, albeit temporarily, appeased.

He moved out of the house a few days after Ruby shot Oswald, so
my teenage laboratory had less opportunity to take note of his psycho-
logical patterns and relative anomalies. But my memories of the earlier
years include visits to the downtown Dallas office where he operated an
entertainment booking agency. A stack of promotional literature for one
Zaney Blaney especially stuck in my mind. Though I never thought to
ask anyone, the mystery lingered for decades. Who is Mr. Blaney and
what makes him "zaney"? The answer came only recently, when I was
working on a magazine article about magicians and came across the
name again.

I learned that Walter "Zaney" Blaney is a prestidigitator who uses
comedy in his act. And in his press pack, along with material detailing
his levitation of Dinah Shore on national television, I found one document that, to me, communicated visually with an "art world" sensibil-
ity. Beneath four portraits, each of equal size, of Walter with Ronald
Reagan, Walter with Richard Nixon, Walter with George H. W. Bush,
and Walter with Gerald Ford, authoritative type proclaimed, "Over the
years four presidents have used Walter Blaney in an advisory capacity."

Variety show ad featuring the Hugh Fowler Orchestra.

Below that, in smaller type, a qualifying statement: "well, sort of an advisory capacity." And below that, in still smaller type, "Okay, to be perfectly honest, the presidents all said, 'Walter, when I want your advice, I'll ask for it.'" With its precise rendering and wry simplicity, the document seemed a fugitive sheet from some museum exhibition of narrative or conceptual art. A work of contemporary art that escaped into the "real" world.

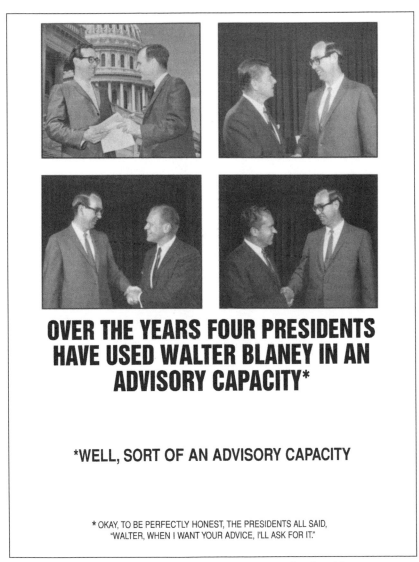

OVER THE YEARS FOUR PRESIDENTS HAVE USED WALTER BLANEY IN AN ADVISORY CAPACITY*

***WELL, SORT OF AN ADVISORY CAPACITY**

* OKAY, TO BE PERFECTLY HONEST, THE PRESIDENTS ALL SAID,
"WALTER, WHEN I WANT YOUR ADVICE, I'LL ASK FOR IT."

Conceptual art found in the "real" world. Courtesy of Walter Blaney.